Kick-Ass Creativity

Kick-Ass Creativity

An Energy Makeover for Artists, Explorers, and Creative Professionals

MARY BETH MAZIARZ

HAMPTON ROADS
PUBLISHING COMPANY, INC.

Cover design by Laura Beers
Cover illustration © Solzick Meister/ImageZoo
Text design by Maxine Ressler
Production Editor: Michele Kimble
Copy Editor: Amy Rost
Proofreader: Susan Hobbs
Typset in Adobe Garamond Pro, Copperplate, and Futura BT

Hampton Roads Publishing Company, Inc.
Charlottesville, VA 22906
www.hrpub.com

ISBN: 978-1-57174-621-4
Library of Congress Cataloging-in-Publication Data available upon request.

Printed on acid-free paper in Canada
TCP

10 9 8 7 6 5 4 3 2 1

To Mark and Daisy, the two loves of my life

DEFINITION: KICK-ASS (KIK´AS´)
adjective

1. having a strong effect on someone or something; forceful; powerful
2. exceptionally good; spectacular, impressive, etc.

—*Webster's New World College Dictionary*

CONTENTS

INTRODUCTION

Why This, Why You, Why Now?

This book is in your hands because you are ready to take your art and creativity to a new level, a greater place in your life. This is exciting and significant. You are already further along in your creative journey than you were just moments ago! Get ready and hold on tight, 'cause it's gonna be a rockin' trip. We're going to have fun. You're going to be shocked at what you can accomplish and how quickly the sense of *forward motion* will start feeling like a regular part of your art and life.

You may have suspected that there's more to your abilities and creative impact than you've been able to demonstrate, which is why there's that nagging ache to devote more time, more page, more thought to the sparks of inspiration that touch you. You *know* you have contributions to make, innovations to birth, light to shine. You sense there's a kick-ass artist/adventurer/discoverer inside of you, and it's dying to get out. I agree! Let's not waste a single second. Let's set that sucker free! There's amazing work to be done, inventions to be

released, delight to find in both process and result. You are a big, wild, fantastic *powerhouse* with important work to do! And in case you're concerned, please trust that you *already have* everything you need to get exactly where you want to go. (You've actually *had it all along*—remember those wise words from Glenda the Good Witch of Oz?) It may be that you just need a little reminding, a little guidance here and there, to nudge you onto the gorgeous currents of the creative jet stream that's right there waiting for you. Let's build enough momentum to lift you off the ground and up into the big creative flow where you can really fly.

Positive forward movement will help pull you out of areas of inertia and unproductive habit. You'll break out of patterns that have kept you from really hitting your stride. There's a place in the mosaic of artistic possibility where we can all say, "Yes! Here I am! I'm bustin' loose! I see *fear* over there, and *responsibilities* and *inexperience* over there, and sure, eighteen other reasons I could decide to wait a little longer before leaping into real progress with my creative work, but I'm not waiting anymore!" The underlying message of this place is clear: it's *time*.

We'll be delving deep into lots of questions about *you*. Who are you? What do you want? Where are you in your artistic journey? Where would you like to really pump things up in your life and process?

You may be a painter, photographer, dancer, writer, actor, or musician. Or perhaps you're a graphic designer, advertising exec, innovative marketer, or architect. Maybe you love to scrapbook, make your own greeting cards, write the family holiday letter, or crochet beautiful blankets for gifts. Or you might assemble gorgeous meals, build cool things that solve problems around your household, or be the go-to person at work when someone needs just the right wording for something. These all count (as do the hundreds of other examples of artistry not listed here).

Maybe you're not sure where to even start or where a creative breakthrough might take you, but you just have a feeling that it's time to begin.

And it is—the time is now for all of us. Your life is a work of art. *Living is a creative act.* We are all creating every day, in all kinds of ways—we merely forget to witness the resonance of our creations as the rhythms of life become regular. Add in the typical responsibilities and distractions of modern life, and creativity starts to feel like a special, decadent dessert instead of our daily bread. It happens gradually, quietly, as our choices become habits, and saving time starts taking precedence over saving our artistic inclinations. Then suddenly, without warning or note, we are flatlining—living, but not alive. This is *not* the kick-ass life we've glimpsed for ourselves in our most free and imaginative moments. We can do better.

So here we are. This is probably not the first book on creativity that you've read, which is good—there's a lot to discuss about creating! There are incredibly valuable books and programs out there that can help us through the step-by-step basics of creating, finding inspiration, recovering our creative spirits, and getting past the fear and anxiety of doing the work. We'll touch on these topics, but to be honest, it would feel repetitive (and derivative) to go into them in depth here. Instead, this book is about taking things to the next level, about bravely looking further into ourselves and our spirits, disrupting the status quo, and feeling thrilled with the results of our efforts. We'll move from where we are now to where we want to be with as much speed, fun, and ease as possible. We're going to reach down deep and pull up the part of us that is *fearless.* We'll uncover and illuminate that powerhouse within us that is pulsing with great ideas, chomping at the bit to create and make a big damn mark on this world! Yeah!

So let's let go, get free, lift out of the "shoulds" and indecision and start moving. Our spirits are at stake. Empowered creativity feeds the soul in specific, revitalizing ways, filling us with animation and direction. Your efforts will make a difference in your whole life (and the lives of those around you). There will be shifting. The tectonic plates that hold your life in place may move around a bit. But things will all shake out in great new ways. The personal

contentment that comes with creative fulfillment allows us to extend terrific generosity of spirit and resources to those around us, making for more harmonious relationships and a more peaceful world. We serve the planet (and our neighborhoods, kids, and partners) by answering our creative urges. You owe it to yourself—and to those you love—to heed the call of your art! It's practically a moral imperative to get your creative juices flowing.

And besides, you'll soon see that you're not just creative, you're *kick-ass creative.* Please forgive the base language, but it's true: inside you is one bold *mother,* all right, undaunted and generous, glowing with excitement and power in all the stages of the creative birthing process. Your brilliant ideas are waiting for you to act! And you can do it! You'll find all the tools you need right here (well, you actually already have them, but I'll help remind you how to use them). You're ready.

And so our energy makeover begins. If this were a TV show, you'd be the "before" picture right now. So if you're feeling particularly bedraggled, that's great! You know that they always try to make people look extra bad at the beginning so they can sparkle with even more glamour at the big reveal.

Our energy makeover will entail adopting some specific ways of thinking and directing our focus. We'll use guidance from everywhere: spiritual laws, psychology, shamanism, life coaching, ancient exotic cultures, and the traditions of artists who've come before us. Some of it will be challenging, some natural, some so much fun you'll wonder where it's been all your life.

First, we'll approach things from a purely energetic side—we'll examine *what energy is, why it matters, and how it affects us.* We'll delve into the physical nature of energy, what it has to do with art, and how opening ourselves up to higher sources of energy can dramatically invigorate the creative process.

Next, we'll learn to work with *the most powerful energy amplifiers (and drains)* in our lives. We'll look the power of desire and feelings in new ways. I can almost hear you now: "Desire? I've already got desire out the wazoo! But feelings? What's the big whoop about feelings!?" It will become clear that feelings both reflect and direct the trajectory of our daily actions and inspiration in astonishing ways. We'll learn to cultivate specific productive feeling states, and become much more conscious of the corresponding energy that we absorb and send out each day. We'll use feeling-awareness techniques like shifting, flipping, and allowing, and we'll play fun games with ourselves, like "finale thinking"; "Well, at least . . ." scenarios; advance "reviews"; and new kinds of journaling. We'll also take a good long look at *balancing* our energy when needed, so we can better know when to charge things up for alignment or step out of the way to allow the universe to do its thing.

Lastly, we'll get into the nuts and bolts of creating and finding fulfillment. We'll use our energy tools to help you get what you most want from your work. We'll discover exactly where you might be getting snagged or drained, and figure out how to get you moving forward. You want better ideas? More groundbreaking flashes of brilliance? More time? More *money?* We'll open the door to these for you. We'll also get up close and personal with resistance, procrastination, and being ready for your dreamiest Big Gig. We'll get those flimsy excuses dissolved and have you rolling and confident, ready to bust on through any obstacle that's getting in the way of your really kicking some creative ass (even if it's your own).

Sometimes it might feel hard, but it'll be a blast too. You'll laugh. You'll cry. (It'll be better than *Cats!)* Most of all, it will be worth it. Your art is worth it. *You* are worth it.

And you are able. Wherever you might currently reside on the kick-ass creative spectrum—novice or master, dabbler or maven—there is always room for the next spark of brilliance, the next thrilling opportunity that might light us up with excitement. As we approach our highest potential, we find not only rewards, but also the demand to step up and present more of ourselves. I believe we crave this challenge at the core of our being. When life feels lacking—when we start wondering if there isn't *something more*—it's because we sense that we are individually *capable* of more, and we're just not sure how to begin.

By opening this book, you're pushing the start button. You're inviting something new into your creative experience and prying open the heavy door to who and what you are meant to become *next*. You're ready to not only get moving, but also to get cracking! You'll soon be lightened—leaving old parts of you behind as you embrace the new pieces of your future. Your energy will sparkle with potency and possibility. I already feel the buzz of your new projects and progress as they begin picking up steam and excitement all over the globe.

Wherever you are, whoever you wish to be, and whatever kind of artistic or innovative mark you intend to make on this world, please know that I am honored to be part of your journey. I know that we've found each other for a purpose.

Welcome.

Let's do it.

PART ONE

All About Energy

(It's here for good.)

There is a vitality, a life force, an energy,
a quickening, that is translated through you into
action, and because there is only one of you in all
time, this expression is unique.
And if you block it, it will never exist through any
other medium and will be lost.

—Martha Graham (1894–1991)

CHAPTER ONE

Energy Works

A Kick-Ass Creator Lives Within You

Every day you have the potential to make contributions to the universe that no one else can possibly provide. You've got something special to offer. You're *gifted*, even. Creators like you share a gift of trust—in themselves and a higher source. You're one of the brave ones, the bold ones, the ones fearless enough to make huge changes and impacts on the world. You find the time that seems to elude everyone else, you believe in your visions, and you courageously stand beside your works and take the heat or applause, respectively. Let's just say it how it is: you've got it goin' on.

There are other wonderful things about you. You're no stranger to creative energy—how it flows, how it slows, how it occasionally is served by large quantities of caffeine or a new

Maybe you're a freewheeling adventurer who hasn't yet found the perfect niche for your creative yearnings.

relationship. You generally feel like you *get* it, even if you haven't always mastered it. You've probably learned to work with (well, tolerate) your inner critic, the occasional fear of failure (or success), and funky productivity rhythms. You may have even done some energy-enhancing work, like positively affirming yourself, jotting into idea journals, and learning the value of daily clearing rituals, all with good results. It's special and rare what you do. You risk! You sacrifice! You take chances, make choices, and give the time, thought, and effort necessary to carve a place for creation into your daily life, whether as a passion, hobby, or full-time career. Day by day, step by step, you discover and embody the life of an artist. *You are one who creates*. Right? Well, sometimes.

And now, my creator friend, you're here, looking for something.

Maybe you're an emerging or established artist seeking new approaches to finding more clarity and fulfillment in the creative process. Or you might be stuck in a rut, going through the motions but no longer feeling very fired-up about things. Or you've got some aspects of your artistic life flowing like crazy and others that never seem to reach the heights you sense are truly possible. You'll find some methods here—especially some working with focus and mindset—that you might not have seen before in other books about creativity and art. Well, alrighty then. New can be helpful. Your art depends on inspiration and resources; it's my deepest hope that through some fresh techniques, you'll soon find much greater riches of both.

Maybe you're an explorer. Maybe you're a freewheeling adventurer who's enjoyed lots of artistic samplings, but hasn't yet found the perfect niche for your creative yearnings (or you're looking for a new one). Or you might be a "never-ever" who has been preparing to spread your wings for awhile, and you're feeling ready to finally get things rolling. Well, good! There's never been a better moment to nudge your dreams to life! We'll define, plan, and pursue. We'll get you moving and feeling great about it. If you've been hesitating, you'll start wondering what you were waiting for all this time. It's easy to hold our great ideas hostage, or to talk them away until they're only things we might do *someday* or *wanted to do once*, but it's so much more thrilling to free them and watch them take flight. Thank you for having the courage to start the path of what's next. I know what it takes to step out of the comfort zone of the familiar and safe, but I also know the rewards. You will too! I'm so excited for what you're about to discover and experience.

Perhaps you work in a creative profession, and the division between your work and art has gotten a little fuzzy lately. Sometimes it's hard to know whether inspiration or commerce is in the driver's seat; this duality can certainly send you on detours of doubt and indecision. When your art becomes subject to specific parameters or business interests, its potency and passion can drain away, leaving you (and it) feeling stale. Commercial artists must deal with pragmatic concerns, sometimes to the detriment of artistic standards. Perhaps these concerns have caused you to question your identity and skills as a "real artist." In tougher moments, you may have even wryly revised your ideas of success, even as others admired your accomplishments or income. In the chapters ahead, we'll visit these paths, too, and see how to usher in fresh vitality and purpose.

Your desire to create puts you into the unique community known as artists: human beings who are willing to put *ideas into form*.

Or maybe you're just tired. Overwhelmed. Distracted. Disillusioned. Burned out. Maybe somewhere along the line, "real life" took over, and your artistic existence became neglected, withering away into the sorry state it's in now. You remember feeling full of ideas once—crackling with possibility—and you miss that potency. Lately you may have heard a quiet, but insistent, call to create (and perhaps even politely asked it to pipe down, please!), but it's still there, tugging at you during the brief pauses in your busy life.

But wait—maybe you're not so sure. Perhaps you're not at all clear yet on where you are and where you can go with your art. Perhaps while reading the preceding paragraphs you found yourself shaking your head with doubt about your inner kick-ass creator status. Maybe you've never felt quite that powerful (or if you did, that was ages ago and you're feeling artistically shlubby these days). Well, no need to fret. Your desire to create puts you into the unique community known as artists: human beings who are

willing to put *ideas into form*. You may have just a glimmer of the traits described above, but that glimmer gets you in the door. It's not only who you are now, but also who you *aspire to be* that matters. So come on in. We're all family here. Whatever your level or genre (yep, beret or no beret), you are an *artist*.

And art, and artists, thrive on energy. We all know that when our mojo is flowing, we're able to create or channel or apply or connect in ways that bring our best work to light.

So let's learn about energy. Let's take a moment to see how it's already at work all over our lives and creative pieces, and how we can learn to recognize it, play with it, reform it, and make it sparkle for our most kick-ass creative process.

This all might feel very serious and classroomlike for a bit, but stay with me. It'll be quick.

In the Beginning...

What is energy, really? It's a word we hear constantly, in dozens of contexts. We're going to define it here as *a powerful, transformative force*. This definition asks that we accept its nature as threefold:

1. as a fuel supply (as a source of vitality and vigor),
2. as an aid in converting ideas to form (that which helps us adapt inspiration into a piece of art), and
3. as an entity (as in, "may the force be with you").

Energy is recognized in many forms, and it can be categorized as active or potential, physical or ethereal, or even having specific anthropomorphic qualities (frantic, calm, happy). From our earliest moments of existence, we human beings are animated by the powerful, transformative force of energy.

Energy is at work in our lives from the moment microscopic cells begin dividing into what will become *us*. There is an intention that guides human stem cells. They hold the potential to become *anything* in the body (thus their value for medical research), but unobstructed, they somehow—brilliantly—divide over and over until they grow into the organs, tissue, and matter that make up our amazing physical vessels.

Our cells traffic in electricity. Every communication in the body is completed through electric impulse. Information flies across the miles of synapses in our brains and other neural pathways to the billions of cells throughout the body to tell us we're hungry, or we're hurt, or even "Oh yeah, right there!"

Our physical energy is subject to all kinds of elements around us. Circadian rhythms help set our preferred waking and bed times by referencing light and temperature patterns in our environment. Different parts of our brain set our body's idling level to restless, mellow, or anything else, and they adjust as necessary to pump us up when we might need to fly, flee, or give a speech. We purposefully ingest substances in our food, medicines, and beverages to hype us up, calm us down, strengthen our immunity, or release inhibitions.[1] We're told to drink lots of water, and we should—hydration matters more than you might imagine. You know those electric impulses zipping around your cells? They adore the fabulous conductivity of water to keep everything running smoothly. And hydration also keeps about 80 percent of your other organs functioning properly, by the way.

We live with and manage other specific energies, too. Sexual energy and attraction can be one heck of a motivator. (Why, *why,* else in the world would single people begin their evenings out on the town at 10 p.m.?) Each of us holds a unique, individual mental energy and focus that allows us to concentrate for hours at some activities, and leaves us drifting off and bored (or asleep) within minutes of starting other tasks. We experience natural highs and lows in our physical energy and can schedule workouts, meals, breaks, or even naps for when they'll most effectively impact our energy in the ways we desire.

1. Some scholars have even attributed the Age of Enlightenment to the emergence of coffee as the European drink of choice. Before coffee, people drank forms of beer or wine all day; perhaps they were too tipsy to become enlightened.

And then there's the rockin' energy of emotion. As you may have noticed, emotions have a way of providing energetic ups and downs like almost nothing else. I know that for me, at least, a bit of exciting news can get me bouncing off the walls with energy, trumping any kind of physical or mental slump I might be in. Oh yes, we'll be working in depth with our old friend, emotion.

There are more subtle parts of our physical energy anatomy as well, and they've been recognized around the world for ages (since about 2000 B.C.). Chinese medicine centers on channels, or *meridians,* that act as circuits through the body for *qi*—the energy flow or *breath*. Keeping qi flowing in one's body and environment is seen as critical to sustaining health, happiness, and well-being. Hindu Ayurvedic tradition calls the body's energy channels *nadis,* and links life-force energy with physiological processes called the *five pranas,* or *vital currents,* of heart/breath, elimination, vocal sounds, digestion/heat, and the voluntary muscular systems. Those who practice yoga or certain forms of meditation may also be familiar with *chakras,* energy centers located throughout the body. The word *chakra* is literally translated as "wheel" or "disk," and chakras are described as brightly colored orbs of spinning energy that correspond to specific body parts and aspects of one's life. Whatever we choose to call these subtle energy channels and life-force energies, getting them clear and flowing within us will be part of our energy makeover.

We've clearly got energy all over the place—in our cells, our minds, our social systems, even all these energetic superhighways throughout our bodies (whether we knew about them or not). But beyond the various types of vibrating frequencies that affect one's daily existence, there is something more that animates us at individual and universal levels. We are spirits. We have consciousness. We are aware. We can connect with a greater source that lifts our potential to heights we may have never imagined for ourselves. This greater source shifts us into kick-ass gear *way* more quickly than we ever could achieve on our own. It also holds all the energy we need to refresh and reform our creative mojo throughout the makeover process and for a full, vibrant lifetime of creating.

Will I Need Crystals?

The moment the word *energy* gets cozy with words like *intention* or *source* or *consciousness,* I know a few of you will wonder if I'm going to get all cosmic on you. Certainly, some recent works have created a mystique about energy work that shrouds it in "secret ancient texts" or mysticism. If you enjoy that type of thing—as I kind of do, by the way—well, great; it can be fun way to approach things and lend some unique dimension to one's daily rhythms. But you should also know that energy dynamics reach far beyond any supposedly woo-woo secrets: this is physics—quantum physics, actually.

Since the turn of the century, physical science has increasingly supported the relationship among energy, vibration, and the effects of conscious focus. (Strangely, we never discussed manifesting desires in my high school science classes; I imagine I might have perked up if we had.) Albert Einstein's Theory of Relativity—probably the only physics theory that most of us can name—describes the relationship between energy and matter, stating that energy and matter are interchangeable. This is *big*. It asks us to revise our understanding of the physical world and to recognize that everything we *know of* is energy. Energy is everywhere, comprising every single thing! It makes up our physical selves and everything around us; it's mutable, flowing, always changing—even in the stuff around us that feels so solid, still, and permanent.

Quantum physics also asserts that everything in the universe—everything—*vibrates.* This is even bigger news. We are engulfed in an all-encompassing interactive matrix of individual energy fields—all day, every day, all around us, vibrations are being absorbed, emitted, shifted, expanded, and merged. (Whew! I know—heavy.)

It's kind of hard to wrap one's brain around the reality of our physical items vibrating, but I think we can find illustrative evidence of it in our lives sometimes. I waited tables in college, and again and again I noticed an interesting seating phenomenon. If patrons were offered their choice of any table in an empty dining

room, *they usually chose the table that had been most recently occupied*. Throughout a shift, a few tables would be occupied by four or five different parties, one after another, while dozens of other tables remained unseated the whole time. Even when hostesses tried to purposefully spread patrons out around the dining room, diners would ask to move to the hotspots! Additionally, I'd find that people with strong emotional states (very lovey-dovey or aggressive toward each other, for instance) would choose tables with the same vibrational imprint as that of earlier patrons. By the end of a busy night, I'd find myself mentally referring to my tables as "chronically angry table" or "bored couple table." There were definitely vibes at work.

Things hold energy.

People Are Plugged In

Each person, place, thing, and idea has an individual variable frequency, almost like our own personal spots on a universal radio dial.

How do humans fit into the vibrational picture? People generate energy frequencies into a spectrum known as the human electromagnetic field. (This is the same vibrational zone inhabited by communication devices like cell phones, radios, and televisions, by the way.) These fields emanate around us like precisely tuned clouds of energy, and they are affected by and included in everything about *us*: our thoughts, our things, our bodies, and our artistic instruments.

Each person, place, thing, and idea has an individual variable frequency, almost like our own personal spots on a universal radio dial. When we use conscious focus, the clarity and intensity of our thoughts and feelings amplifies our energy field in measurable ways. Energy literally *expands around us*, vibrationally testing the waters nearby to determine if we'd like to engage with the energy of some other person, place, thing, or experience. Our energy speaks to us.

Finally, there are a dozen other laws of physics that support you on your energetic artistic path. Modern science accepts and avows the following:

1. Nothing in this world is fixed. (We don't need to be stuck or blocked.)
2. There are no limitations. (Our desires are not limited by circumstance, time, or anything else.)
3. There are no separate parts of the universe. (We're not trying to weave this thing together on our own; it's already all connected.)
4. Everything exists in a fluidlike form, always shifting, ever available, flowing one part into the next without boundaries. (Responses can be instantaneous and fuller than we can possibly imagine. Things aren't as linear as they look; the puzzle pieces are already put together in finished form somewhere.)
5. We are all part of each other, both through our common experience and our actual atomic construction. (There's no reason for competition or lack; we all have unlimited resources and opportunities.)

From a very literal standpoint, *art is full of vibrations*—tonal frequencies, spectrum light wavelengths, rhythm patterns.

As you can see, the work of Einstein and his pals supports you every step of the way. (Take *that*, skeptical Aunt Martha.)

What's Energy Got to Do With Art?

Most of us found our way to art without any big awareness of energy, didn't we? We may have started with a little natural talent, developed some skills, and decided that making art was more fun than not making art, right? A fairly straightforward equation. So what's energy have to do with it?

From a very literal standpoint, *art is full of vibrations*—tonal frequencies, spectrum light wavelengths, rhythm patterns. So in theory, we're already increasing our alignment with naturally pure, high vibrations, just by working with art itself. For instance, playing a musical instrument affects bodily systems in marked ways,

such as lowered blood pressure, a slower and more regular heart rate, and increased release of the relaxing neurotransmitters serotonin and melatonin. Do these results take place due to thoughts experienced while playing or because of the soothing physical vibrations traveling through the strings or keys onto one's fingers or body? Researchers continue to debate the causes, but the effects remain quantifiable (and remarkable).

I suspect that artists and creatives *feel* energy more viscerally than the average person, so the contact with specific sources of energy and vibration gives us more buzz than the average Joe. We frequently do it with the physical tools of our art. I'm not suggesting that there's a palpable electric jolt when you pick up the camera or start mixing the paints, but how often does a writer prefer a certain pen, chair, or typewriter to help get the juices flowing? How many musicians have intense connections with their instruments, even to the point of naming them? Vibes matter to artists.

Artists notice energy in spaces and groups, too. Dancers talk about the live, crackling energy of a premiere studio or the hushed vibe of a revered stage. Sculptors note the presence (or lack thereof) in a piece when it is installed in a particular space. Actors frequently describe audiences as "dead" or "on fire." Sure, some artistic idiosyncrasies are driven by superstition or habit, but I think it's also reasonable to imagine that the physical items, works, and spaces in our artistic lives carry vibrations that we recognize at some level.

I'm a pianist and songwriter in another part of my creative life, and when I decided to purchase a grand piano several years ago, I imagined it would be a straightforward process. I'd designate my budget, spend a few days visiting the piano stores in our area, play a few dozen instruments, and choose the one to have delivered to the house. Instead, I discovered that I had a significant journey ahead of me.

It took me *nine months* to find the perfect instrument (my grand-piano gestation period, apparently). I played every piano in my price range (and above) within a day's drive. I searched eBay. I scoured online classifieds daily. (Admittedly, at the time I was not versed in getting my energy aligned with what I wanted, so the process was probably much slower and more labor intensive than it needed to be.)

Finally, I found my piano: a gorgeous, well-played, seven-foot Mason & Hamlin from 1928. I knew it was mine immediately. I felt comfortable, easy, relaxed as I played it. It felt like home. It was just the perfect mix of well preserved and well used, and I just knew I could work well on this wonderful instrument. After finally getting it settled into our house, I found out the piano's history and felt an even deeper connection. For its entire life—from the time it was delivered from the factory back in 1928—it had been owned by the same family. This one family, over four generations, had played it often and loved the instrument. I think the piano held onto that loving, affectionate vibration and was somehow waiting for someone like me, who would play it daily and love it deeply too.

Power to the Pieces

Passionate debate keeps the question "what is art?" healthily alive, but for our purpose, I offer the following response to it: *art is an embodied form of energy*. Energy fuels the process of art's inspiration and creation, and in turn, art acts as the carrier for an idea, the vehicle for energy from the etheric to the physical realms. Without energy, we merely have gesture, phrase, or line without meaning or resonance. Art begins and ends with energy—it's energy that ignites the first small spark of a concept within its maker and energy which resonates with lasting reverberations in those who experience the work. It's the captured energy in art that can spur an emotional reaction: our personal vibration aligns with that of the piece and voila! We have contact. We are affected, *moved*. We have been changed, in some major or small way.

Energy has inhabited art since men and women began making marks, shapes, movements, and sounds as a way to chronicle, interpret, and affect their mysterious worlds. Early cultures swirled the sacred into art, using paintings, totems, and sculptures as pleas

to the gods, preparation for the hunt, or gestures of thanks to elemental deities. Ceremonies of native peoples, even today, feature dance and song as ways to lift away from bodily concerns into the world of the spirit. Ancient Greeks connected music with the power to heal the body, and their use of archetypical characters and a chorus style of theater still informs modern playwriting.

Art has served as an agent of change. Social commentary and call for reform often emerges first and most persuasively from the artistic community before taking hold in the mainstream. Through energy-rich artistic forms like song, illustration, poetry, photography, and oration, artists have been able to tell the stories of their generations and effect powerful, progressive change.

Modern commerce has paid attention to all this powerful, energy-rich art, and happily put it to use in garnering the public's attention and dollars. In the last thirty years, the advertising world has dramatically blurred the line between artistic and commercial. Pop songs about social responsibility are used to advertise running shoes. Billboards, renegade art, and urban spray-paint murals compete with each other for our notice and admiration (and all sometimes earn it). Hip, creative graphics and pithy quotes appear on our water bottles and coffee cups. Catalogs read like magazines.

New forms of energy flood our lives and creative processes every day. Computers allow us to write, record music, design graphics, edit images, find information, and communicate in ways we couldn't have fathomed a few decades ago. We take (pretty darn good) photos with our cell phones. We share our thoughts and whereabouts with huge online communities in a few keystrokes. Our sewing machines can stitch the alphabet all by themselves, for goodness sakes! Art is available everywhere—even in the ether, as we wirelessly, instantly download and browse songs, images, books, and whatever else we can imagine.

State of Our Art

As we examine our current creative climate in relation to our energy reserves and needs, questions arise. Fantastically exciting and advanced tools are available to us in almost every artistic field, yet has all this technology made us better artists? Have we become a hundred times as prolific as our artistic ancestors with their painstaking, time-consuming techniques?

We're certainly not at a loss for information. Every conceivable thought ever laid to paper is available in some form almost instantaneously these days. Has this ease of reference and accessibility allowed us all to make leaps and bounds of creative brilliance?

Even time is on our side, supposedly. Workers in the 1800s put in seventy-two hour workweeks and headed back to additional strenuous, time-consuming work at home. With fewer hours at our jobs and the host of modern conveniences we enjoy around our homes, do we find ourselves with plenty of time to spend on the activities that we love?

With all this innovation and opportunity, we all must be exactly as inspired, supported, prosperous, appreciated, balanced, well known, and thrilled as we want to be, right?

Finally, we're barraged with thousands of media messages each day about how to live more healthily, abundantly, spiritually, romantically, and beautifully. Self-help programs are more popular than ever, abounding in every bookstore and talk-show segment. There are literally millions of outlets for creative products and services—more than ever before—and the closed-door policies that many creative industries used to espouse have been flung wide open by independent, agile companies trying things in new ways. Supposedly, everything we need to be out there, making our mark, is right here for us. We're awash with opportunity.

On paper, there's never been a better time to be an artist.

So, with all this innovation and opportunity, we all must be kick-ass creative already, right? Surely we're all exactly as inspired, supported, prosperous, appreciated, balanced, well known, and thrilled as we want to be, right? Right?

Well...

Although we may keep up a pleasant, positive attitude for non-artist friends, family, and acquaintances, the answer for most of us is often something a little more like, "Not really."

So what gives? Why is the artistic life so frustrating sometimes? Sure, we do it because we *love the work*—of course we do. But more and more often, other concerns creep in and degrade the

creative satisfaction that somehow used to be enough. Why are we so tired? So "over it?" Can't we do better for ourselves? Where is all the energy that our modern world supposedly affords us? We work with creativity all the time, don't we? Are we not creative enough to find the strategies and resources to make things really happen for us?

While we're at it, is it even *possible* to have a fantastically satisfying creative path? Can we find a way to develop a life full of what we really want instead of seeing it evade us? Can we remain true to personal ideals while still enjoying the pleasures of life, such as supportive, nurturing relationships and abundant incomes? Is it all right to crave (and get) recognition and validation for our works?

Um—yes.

Yes! Of course it is! (Wait, am I sure? *Yes!*)

So how do we get there?

Let's start by observing our creative process from the *inside out*, taking some time to look at what happens *before* a piece comes to life. Instead of immediately jumping into how to improve the techniques of our chosen form or how to get better response to our finished products, we can examine and start nurturing what *feeds* our process. It's kind of like our need for clean water. We can boil and purify and treat water that comes from uncertain origins, and it'll get us by, or *we can find a better source.* Water that's flowing and pure, sparkling and fresh, brings with it sensory delights and gifts far beyond the basic needs it fills.

We find a better source for our creative refreshment (and those pesky basic needs) by tapping into the higher, richer flow of inspiration available to all of us. We can begin to see how we are creative portals for brilliance, scribes for ideas grander than we might imagine all by our individual selves. We can acknowledge that there is an underlying mosaic *(or "muse-aic")* of inspiration within every creative piece, of which we are only *one* part. We can forge a clearer partnership with the knowing force that helps us connect the many disparate wisps we piece together into the fully realized inventions, songs, stories, campaigns, performances, or presentations of our own hands.

When we're connected to this source, *cool things happen*. It's as if all of a sudden, fate decides to start helping us out. Synchronicity occurs. Opportunities arise. The things we need, whether big or small, appear with perfect—almost freaky—timing. We overhear a conversation with exactly the information we've been seeking. We pull up to find a rock-star parking spot waiting for us. We're inspired to look behind the desk and discover the exact book that we need right now. We note the perfect shade of brown in our morning coffee. We wake up in the night, finally sure of how our novel ends or how to weld the tricky top piece of the sculpture. Each next step feels clear and easy and fun.

When we're connected to this source, the things we need, whether big or small, appear with perfect—almost freaky—timing.

So how do we get this thing going and start collecting the benefits? The simplest way to start is by knowing, then *flowing*, what you want. Pretend, feel, and believe that you're experiencing the results of your desires *already*—or recognize the little bits of them already in your life and get expanding them, baby!—and you'll begin cultivating the energy of what you want and attracting more of it.

A lot of artists in my life share my affection for the jump-right-in-now-and-sort-out-the-details-later approach to things. Why don't we take a little test drive to see how to put our energy to work for us.

Good, 'Cause I Need Something Now!

First, we need to define something that would feel really exciting for you. Do you already know what would make you most happy with your art right now? It could be anything—fulfillment appears in a different outfit for each of us.

Maybe it's about experiences. Would you like a more flowing—make that a *kick-ass*—creative process? The satisfaction of seeing your pieces beautifully, flowingly coming to life? The status and ego boost of high-profile gigs? The thrill of reading fantastic reviews? The chance to meet or work with your idols? The sense of calm that would come with plenty of time to focus on a big upcoming project?

Perhaps it's more about social and cultural contribution. Would you like more public awareness of your work? Opportunities to mentor and inspire others? A deeper connection with your audiences? Feedback that people find your work deeply moving, or life-changing, even?

Maybe you'd like to make changes to your lifestyle. A more consistent and abundant inflow of money might be nice (and convenient). The ability to pay off some long-term debt might sound pretty great. How about some nice trips to conferences or relaxing vacation spots?

Only *you* know what your heart desires and what you need to feed your spirit and your art.

These feel like a good start, but just for fun, let's think bigger. How about some fabulously large performance fees, big fun advances, and luxurious travel perks? Great new updated gear? An assistant? A dedicated place in which to work, with all the room and privacy you need?

All these things—and many, many more—are available to you. Only *you* know what your heart desires and what you need to feed your spirit and your art. You can attract *absolutely anything* you like in your experience, and the process can be fast and straightforward. (I sense there is a little part of you silently arguing with me right now. "Not everything *I* want," you're saying. But it's true. You can attract *anything*.) There is a world of goodies out there, great things and feelings and experiences, waiting on *you*.

Now pick one thing that sounded fun for you while reading the possibilities above. Or you can name a desire that's not on the list, of course.

Got it? Good.

Uh oh. Wait. Before we even have begun really working on what you want, you may have noticed your brain starting to whirl on the series of nots: It's not realistic. It's not possible. I'm not good enough. It might not be that great if it happened anyway. I'm sure you can imagine how these nots are not helpful.

So here's a better angle for you: figuring out the how, when, and where of what you want is not your job. The universe is a much better

master planner than you or I could ever be. So for now, let's release the whirling nots (or knots) and move into the realm of the flowingly fantastically possible.

Free of any clingy nots? Good.

Now let's imagine you've been instantly transported to a moment where *you've just experienced* the crux of your chosen desire. You've just deposited a massive royalty check, walked off the stage of an amazing gig, finished the most luminous painting you've ever done, or completed *whatever* your particular desire is at this moment. You're right in the thick of it, and it's amazing! It's real. You're right there. And it's better than you'd even thought!

Yes, okay now, deep breath. And we're back in happy fulfilled-desire land.

Unless it isn't. This feels like a good time to mention that we'll have no negative drama or hassles in our vision and feeling work. Make up good, exciting sensory elements, please—this is your shindig. Set up your ideal situation, not what you might think is a "realistic" (or pessimistic) rendering of how this desire might feel in your life. No money-grubbing relatives, friendless weekends, pending divorces, or kids going off to juvy due to their absent parents, please. The whole idea is about figuring out exactly what you'd really enjoy, not visualizing your dream gig fraught with issues, for goodness sakes.

Yes, okay now, deep breath. And we're back in happy fulfilled-desire land.

Sense the details first: What are you doing? What's the environment like? What can you hear? What do you touch or taste or smell? Who else is there? This exercise is about using your imagination, so if you don't know what the sensory elements would be, go ahead and make them up.

Now take a quick inventory of what you *feel*. Are you glad? Relaxed? Relieved? Proud? Psyched? Energized? Delighted? Overwhelmed with gratitude? Do you feel lucky? Abundant? Generous? Whatever it is, take note and allow yourself to just float wonderfully in this terrific feeling.

Stay here for a minute. Close your eyes and breathe deeply as you continue to experience the feelings resulting from receiving what you desire. (Mmm! Now isn't that nice?)

Excellent. Did you feel a little lift, a little excitement at the possibility of having something you really want? Did you feel a tiny carbonated rush in your gut or find a little unexpected smile on your face? Maybe you noticed that you sensed just a bit more hope, or relief, or trust toward your art or ideas. If so, you've begun tapping into the flow, the greater source. You've activated gorgeous, focused energy on your behalf, paving the way for your desire to come into your life. At the heart of it, what we're going to do throughout the rest of this book is *that* simple. Yes, there's more to it—there are lots of ways to get energy working for you more often, easily, intensely, and powerfully, and we're going to explore many of them. But if you had to pinpoint the most basic way of accessing higher energy and pulling what you really want into your life, this is it: *you gotta feel it.*

Our desires begin really taking off when we find a way to experience what we *feel* as our hopes come to fruition.

Our desires begin really taking off when we find a way to experience—in advance, at some level—what we *feel* as our hopes come to fruition. This turns the tiny little spark of your want into a veritable flare, sending out a kind of beacon to the powers-that-be that you're ready, willing, and able to accept whatever it is you desire in your life. By really embodying the feeling of what you hope to experience, you indicate that it's *already here* in some way for you—you're just magnifying the feelings already present in you.

Of course it's possible you had a little trouble getting into the feeling just now. Maybe some unexpected things came up that you *don't* want to amplify, like some fear, or anxiety, or a sense of being overwhelmed. That's okay. This whole book is about how energy works and how to apply it more effectively to your artistic life. If you were already experiencing everything you wanted, you probably wouldn't be seeking new insights about bringing your dreams and goals to fruition. You're here to figure that out. So now you have a starting place that you can reference as you find out more detail and develop great skills. That's something. Very good, artist.

Ready for Your Energy Close-Up?

Now we're ready to start the exercises that will form the structure for your energy makeover. Each chapter in Part One will include a few questions about the chapter topic, a Bonus Kick-Ass Challenge, and an Opening the Flow Project Rec—recommendation, that is—for those wanting to bust out of their ruts or sticky spots as quickly as possible. (There's also an alternate Crazy-Easy Route for the super-overwhelmed among us.) The exercise tasks will bring more energy awareness to your current creative endeavors and daily rhythms, and offer hands-on opportunities for applying new tools as they're introduced. Each chapter of Part Two will conclude with a Creative Soul Search—a series of questions to help you dissolve creative blocks and discover practical ways to free up more time and energy.

Go at your own pace—the timeline is up to you. You could methodically spend a week on each chapter, linger on each section until you feel ready to move on, or read through the whole thing and settle back in where you feel especially jazzed (or freaked out) by the questions and exercises. You can write your answers and Project Rec discoveries right here in the margins, in a blog online, or even in a spanking new journal chosen just for this occasion. (Ooh! I love brand-new notebooks!) If you prefer to be more tactile than verbal, you might choose to jot down the basics verbally and then supplement your answers in another form that sounds fun. (That's it! Rock some coffee-stain drawings! Drip some candle wax onto those pages! Get out that funky Lomo! Make up a song or dance or character that adds depth to the exercise for you! Anything you'd like to use to further explore or play will benefit the process.)

Please be ridiculously honest with yourself as you approach questions and tasks, even if it occasionally makes you feel like kind of a mess. (Remember, we're looking at some significant "before-picture" stuff in many of these tasks.) We've all been there, on both extremes of the creative ass-kicking spectrum, so there's no need to

be self-conscious or embarrassed. Allow yourself to unfold authentically, organically, as you prepare to grow and lift off. We show the most progress when we've come the farthest distance; the more modest our roots, the more transcendent our flight will be.

You know you've got it in you. I know you do too.

Chapter One: Energy Works

Your before shot awaits. How do you look, energetically? (No sugar-coating necessary here.) What *aren't* you getting that you really, really want?

1. Where are you experiencing the most frustration with your energy right now? Is it primarily physical? Mental? Lack of inspiration? Blocks with your process? Disappointing levels of response? Not enough resources? Make a list of everything that's not working.

2. What's going on now in your life that might be inhibiting your energy?

3. Describe your typical day in terms of energy. You can chart out the day in hours, then mark your highs and lows, if you like. What kinds of things do you do to affect your energy? Do they work?

____

____

____

____

____

* **BONUS KICK-ASS CHALLENGE:** *Why* do I want to change my creative (and any other) energy? After you've written down your answer, ask yourself this in follow up: and why do I want *that?*

____

____

____

____

____

OPENING THE FLOW

PROJECT REC: Draw a picture outline of your body (not life size—unless you want to, you fabulous thing!) and use color, glitter, dirt, feathers, or anything else to illustrate areas where you feel most potent (or blocked) energetically. Express your strengths and congestion with patterns, textures, phrases—anything you like. Do you feel your hands know what to do, but your mind doesn't? Or vice versa? Is your heart not "in it?" There's no right or wrong. Just let yourself create as accurate a rendering as you can. For extra credit, create and leave your portrait in a natural, outdoor environment. After twenty-four hours pass, come back and revisit your portrait. How has it changed? How have you?

Crazy-Easy Route: The next time you notice yourself affected energetically by a feeling (maybe fatigue, boredom, frustration, excitement), take a second to notice your physicality. How is your posture? Are you still or moving? Is there a place in your body where you notice the feeling centered? Does it have a texture or color or rhythm to it (buzzing, pulsing, plodding, etc.)? No crayons needed. Just notice it. And notice if *the noticing* does anything to the feeling itself.

CHAPTER TWO

Big Creative

Being part of a piece coming to life—participating in its journey from the spark of an idea into form—offers one of life's most exciting (and possibly addictive) sensory and psychologically rewarding experiences. You've felt it, right? That fantastic, sparkly rush in your gut, the whole-body shower of goose bumps, the smile that won't leave your face as you realize: Something is happening here! I like this piece—it's working! This is going to be really cool! When we're in that gorgeous moment of certainty, of confident creating, we are true believers. We are on fire, connected, grounded and flying at once.

Other times, we feel a million miles away from inspiration or brilliance. We're certain we've never done anything significant, and worse yet, we never will. We wonder at the time we've already wasted on the whole thing.

Or maybe we think we're onto something exciting, and we suddenly fall flat. We discover that our most recent brilliant idea is already in progress in someone *else's* artistic life. (Google and I have had some heartbreaking moments with that one.) A wayward word from a confidante leaves us deflated. Or it's less obvious than that, more internal, as if our unfolding inspirational flow somehow got cut off and abruptly the powerlines went down. We feel cold, flailing, awkward, doubtful. Worried. Alone.

How do we get off this roller coaster? Is it possible to nurture a more resilient connection to that highest creative state? How can we strengthen our resolve for a lifetime, not just the next project (or this afternoon's session)? How do we fill our energy reserves with the *real stuff*, not just temporary fixes or hopped-up highs that leave us quickly crashing and depleted again?

How do we get off this roller coaster? Is it possible to nurture a more resilient connection to that highest creative state?

It's tempting to believe we can *muscle* our way to insane levels of discipline, to force ourselves by sheer will into models of productivity and inspiration, but let's be honest. Haven't we already tried this method? Haven't we jacked ourselves up on whatever we thought might work in the past and found that it still let us down? All the caffeine, sugar, alcohol, drugs, schedules, deadlines, inspiring quotes, goal sheets, and artist groups in the world can't keep us going indefinitely.

Some people seem to *always* be creating; they're having a blast, doing great work, allowing one project to lead beautifully and organically to the next, and all with a spring in their step. They mention amazing coincidences and fun synergy. Their processes look easy, almost effortless; statements like, "I just had an idea, and I did it" come up frequently (much to the chagrin of those struggling at the moment). Furthermore, they gather rewards and attention that so many of us crave.

What's their secret? There *must* be something more, something really special, that invigorates and strengthens these models of kick-ass creativity we admire and envy and aspire to be. Were they *born* this way, into a charmed artistic existence? Did they have all kinds of advantages growing up that allowed their full potential to come to life? Do they have some secret habits or tools (special vitamins? a qi gong master? a supersweet, lightning-fast laptop?) that keeps them on this higher creative plane?

Maybe you've gotten close to breaking through to this powerhouse kind of energy, but feel you've still missed the mark. You may have gotten to the point where you can bop out of your seat with physical vitality, feel mentally sharp as a tack, and know you've got great friends and a wonderfully centered, content existence, yet still sense that there is something critically important *missing* in your life, pulsing somewhere deep beneath the day-to-day maintenance and pleasantries. This is the call of our fullest potential, and I think most of us desperately want to embody it, as frightening as that path might sometimes seem.

The path of finding this potential asks that we open up and connect our intimate, immediate self with our highest one. We can find that elusive "something more" and expand it into something huge and thrilling in our very own lives. We can start listening, and honor the call of Big Creative.

The Fountainhead of Inspiration

Within each of us is a consciousness that is both human and divine: this is the energy of the *soul.* We are more than tumbling atomic particles, more than instinct and evolution in action. We are awake to our being, which makes us rich with both possibility and responsibility. We hold the ability to plan, to design, to imagine, to intend. We can feel. We can choose. And we can *focus,* directing our attention to that which we seek and allowing the rest to fall aside. We can invite the higher power of our choice—and understanding—to journey with us or come to our aid.

When we're open to this higher power, this source, we become channels to great brilliance, to ideas beyond our own scope. It's here that our spirits are fueled and that energy takes on both a distinctly personal and universal tone. One might call this source God, the Universe, our Expanded Self, the Great Creator, even just Source with a special capital S—anything you want, really. Use any

term or understanding that feels right for you and go with it in a way that hopefully leaves you free of any baggage or unproductive associations. (This is about connecting with your highest, best self, not any certain philosophy or dogma.)

When we are in open contact with Big Creative, our spirits lift, and we bump up against the divine.

I believe that the real adventure of art-making, that intricate combination of leap and surrender, begins on a wondrous tide of energy and ideas that springs eternal from the Great Source, the river of radiant potential. It's larger than life, grander than us, yet we have access to it anytime we chose: it's *Big Creative.* Big Creative is the massive current of inspiration that is available to us anytime, anywhere. Big Creative gushes with thrilling ideas, moving art, and brave new innovation. Big Creative welcomes us to dip in with hefty cups, take a deep drink, bathe in it, love in it, delight in it.

When we are in open contact with Big Creative, we are meditation in action—wakeful and calm, but with our hands or mouths or whole bodies knowing what to do. Our spirits lift, and we bump up against the divine, bridging the gap between the world of ideas and the world of the physical. Often the result of this meeting of worlds is *brilliance.*

Big Creative fills our tanks like no other fuel imaginable. And the best part is that there's no lack, no competition—there's plenty of everything for everyone. There's not even a skills or worthiness requirement before one is allowed to tap on into Big Creative. There need only be a few things, and they're already parts of our everyday lives.

The first is *focus.*

WTF? ("What's the Focus?" That Is)

What does it mean to focus?

For our purposes, it means putting our awareness and attention squarely on what we *want,* whether for our creative projects, the world, or ourselves. It means consciously choosing *not* to linger on what we *don't want,* or to spend our time and energy on worry, blame, or anything else that makes us feel like crap. It also means getting honest and noticing what's not working so we can start moving toward what *we do* want, since it's positive focus that opens us up to Big Creative and keeps us connected to the highest sources of inspiration and energy.

Next we'll want to bring in *desire, feelings, alignment*, and *allowing*.

You know how desire basically works, right? It starts with a feeling. You decide (often subconsciously) that you want a certain *feeling*, and then you direct your actions toward getting the thing, person, or experience you imagine will *bring you that feeling*. Desire is like our destination—it's where we've decided we want to go.

Feelings act as our compass as we move in the direction of our desire.

Feelings act as our compass as we move in the direction of our desire. They're like a GPS device guiding us to what we want, and they're calibrated by the qualities of our emotions, good and bad. Feelings give us immediate feedback on how we're progressing. Good feelings tell us we're getting warmer—that we're hot on the trail toward the things and experiences we want. Bad feelings, unfortunately (but helpfully), tell us just the opposite. Along with the specifics of the sadness, anger, or frustration we might be feeling, negativity also indicates that we're moving *away* from that which will bring our deepest joy.

Alignment is like fuel for our journey; it's what gets things moving fast and powerfully. How do we align ourselves with what we want? What do we *do* to get aligned with Big Creative in our lives? We find real alignment when we get into the full feeling state of our desires, creating really fun buzz and excitement as we imagine the sensory sides of what we want.

Allowing is the state of relaxation and disengagement that asks us to step back for the sake (not detriment) of our desires. In our little journey metaphor, allowing would be the wisdom that pries our cramped hands off the wheel and lets our partner drive for awhile, so we can make better time and get there safely. It's the trust that we don't need to do everything ourselves in order to get where we want to go.

These five elements—focus, desire, feelings, alignment, and allowing—are the most powerful tools we have for making over our energy. They can be the best energy amplifiers and most daunting drains, so we'll need to use them properly and skillfully. We'll look at each one in depth, along with some other helpful techniques, in the next several chapters.

With these tools, we'll navigate the roar and thrust of Big Creative, which will allow it to carry us to places we could never reach on our own, even if we were to paddle diligently for years. Regularly connecting with this awesome Source will get you more of what you want out of *all* your creative endeavors. As with any powerful force, it helps if we work *with* the current rather than against it, so let's explore the dynamics that govern Big Creative.

Go with the Flow

In order to create the opportunity for flow, our goals should be *challenging but attainable.*

How do we know when we're plugged into Big Creative? Do our fingers suddenly leave sparks on the keyboard? Does the pen tingle in our hand? Do we hear voices? (Maybe! But probably not.) Most of us have probably felt the power of Big Creative intuitively sometime in the past, but how can we tell for sure?

One of the best signifiers of a strong connection to Big Creative is the experience of flow. Flow is a state of elevated focus and satisfaction, marked by a sense full engagement that allows us to lose track of time and our environment while taking part in an activity. Many people instinctively find themselves in states of flow while taking part in favorite activities—pastimes such as reading, sports, cooking, gaming, and gardening all can stimulate flow. But flow can also be developed, beckoned, by the way we structure our creative work, according to Mihály Cziksentmihályi in his seminal book on the topic.[2] In order to best create the opportunity for flow, our goals should be *challenging but attainable.* When we're required to stretch, using all our faculties to solve a problem or work on a task, we reach a level of optimal stimulation;

2. Cziksentmihályi, Mihály. *Flow: The Psychology of Optimal Experience.* New York: Harper Perennial Modern Classics, 2007.

we're fully, but not overly, extended. We find a perfect balance of fascination, ability, and motivation, which leads to suspended time and self-awareness. We find the exact sweet spot where tasks are difficult, but not frustrating—doable, but not boring. Deadlines, new media or genres, and the unfolding of different stages within the creative process help stimulate this state of motivated concentration for many artists. The combination of skill-based work and effective pressure creates just the right combination of confidence and uncertainty for flow to occur.

Identifying areas of flow helps us define the richest mines of creative payload.

Additionally, flow thrives in an atmosphere of clearly defined steps and direct, immediate feedback. Knowing what to do next in a project allows us to move forward at a pleasing pace. We edit scenes of our film one after another, then go back and watch them in context to make sure the story makes sense and is unfolding properly. We combine, cook, and spice our food, using several senses to make sure each part of the meal is cooked properly. We sing in a group, listening closely to make sure we're on pitch and on the proper beat.

So we can look at flow in two distinct ways. In its most spiritual context, flow is the touch of the divine, which allows us to suspend our individual consciousness and open to the realm of a bigger, higher creative source working through us. On the physical level, flow is a psychological state of heightened focus in which self-consciousness dissolves, leaving us free to work at the leading edge of our ability in exceptionally fulfilling and effective ways. Either way, it's very good for our creative lives.

Identifying areas of flow—in the past and present—helps us define the richest mines of creative payload. When we fully immerse ourselves in an activity, we are released from the limitations and assumptions of our day-to-day reality. Flow can also serve as a shortcut to just feeling good and getting better aligned with what we want when we feel upset or off-track.

Flow can also help us deal with negative emotion or environmental chaos. As a kid, I loved playing the piano and writing songs, which happily led to music becoming my adult profession. Before I imagined I would pursue it as a career, however, music served

We find unique, pleasing benefits from the *process* of our art that serve us almost as much as the official fruits of our labor.

another purpose for me: it held a pattern of positive reinforcement that had nothing to do with approval or material reward. *It allowed me to find flow on a regular basis.* When playing, I got caught up in the rhythms and melodies, and I lost all track of everything else. I relaxed. I calmed down. I released thoughts of competition or self-consciousness. My mind lifted out of the occasional spirals of frustration that left me depressed and drained. I had found a way to get myself into a more powerful feeling state, which not only made things *feel* better, but also shifted my personal energy in such a way that things started *actually getting* better.

Several years ago, my parents' great home burned down in a furnace-related fire. The grand piano I'd played since I was about eleven years old went down with the house, and upon rebuilding, my folks decided not to replace it. Whenever I'm home now in the "new," but incredibly similar, house, if I feel a little stressed, I'll find myself wandering in the direction of the room where the old piano was—just to play for a few minutes, relax, and take some time for myself. And of course the piano isn't there anymore! So along with the intensity and pandemonium of a big family, holidays, and lots of activity, I also now find myself without my favorite on-ramp to flow! It makes things a little trickier than they used to be when I need a break. (Helloooo, eggnog!)

As a kid, I had stumbled onto a shortcut to the state of flow, and playing the piano gave me some solitude in a lively, chaotic household. I imagine most of us experience beneficial perks—like flow or solitude—from our work. I think we find unique, pleasing benefits from the *process* of our art that serve us almost as much as the official fruits of our labor. Whether conscious or not, I believe most artists actively seek these *process perks* as much as the works themselves. Maybe we crave the quiet, or the escape from stress, or reconnection with a sense of identity that we lose in the busy rhythms of children or business. We seek something important in *the work itself,* something immediate that is not explained by many of the rewards of the finished product. Perhaps our craving includes the longing for *flow* and the energizing touch of Big Creative.

Inviting Big Creative into our process requires that we're open to the concepts that we are stewards for something bigger than ourselves, and that we can welcome this relationship more fully into our lives. We can let go of the exhausting idea that we need to do everything by ourselves, and in this state of surrender, find that our work often shines brighter, comes faster, and resonates more powerfully. This discovery can be strangely disconcerting.

The moment we truly embrace the concept that we are *vessels* for inspiration, not originators, an interesting thing happens: our egos start fighting, hard, for the right to take credit. *I* did this, the ego says. *I* noticed these parts and put them together. *I earned this.* Perhaps we'd be wise to reframe our sense of entitlement to acclaim; perhaps we'd do better to deny the claim that the brilliance was ever ours at all. Instead, we can take full pride and credit for showing up, doing our part, and placing our hands in the starting position, even when we had no idea where it would lead us.

There's no need to publicly give credit to a greater source. (Thankfully, it's not necessary to bang from the rooftops, "Hey y'all! It wasn't me! I got a sweet hookup to Big Creative!") But we can still internally choose to view our creative role from this slightly separated view. If we close off the ego from the creative process, we free ourselves from some of the weight of responsibility that wears us out on these journeys. If I'm not feeling connected or flowing, I can work on *that,* rather than beat myself up for not producing spectacular stuff today. I can rest, feed myself better, meditate, or shift in a dozen other ways. Prying the ego away from the process also leaves less personal, residual static to cloud the work itself. We release the litany of voices in our heads that occasionally tell us it's no good or it's been done or who are you to try this? and let the light shine through us. We can just, as they say, do it.

Woke Up This Morning, and I Wrote Down This Song . . .

When we're connected with Big Creative and creating in an optimal state of flow, work sometimes comes especially quickly and easily. It might feel like taking dictation more than writing. We feel our limbs moving, almost guided, to the right places. The work

seems to fall out of us, fully formed, with little need for editing or reworking.

In these moments, flow allows us to access the "finished" version of a piece before we've actually hammered out the details. Michelangelo talked about *releasing* the statue from the stone. He believed the piece was already there and his job was to merely uncover it. James Taylor speaks of it in his song "Fire and Rain." He sings: "I woke up this morning, and I wrote down this song." He didn't say, "I hemmed and hawed and tried about fifteen different rhymes 'til I finally found some good lines and wrenched this song out of my gut." He says he wrote *down* the song. It was already there somehow. He heard, he heeded, and we now have one of the most popular songs in western music.

Grammy-nominated songwriter Beth Nielsen Chapman talks about sensing details of a finished piece long before it's even clear what's forming. While writing, she often hears the *sounds* of the words as they come through to her; this sense requires her to keep boxes of "song embryo" tapes that she records during the process—bits and pieces of lyric or melody that will someday find a home. She remembers sounding out pieces of the lyric to her song "Sand and Water," having no idea how it would resolve. "Solid stone is just sand and water," she recalled writing. "What does this mean?" she thought. "Where is this going?" But she kept writing, kept listening, kept getting down the pieces. The lyric later came together to create her hugely impactful and moving song about grief.

That, dear artists, is *faith*. Faith keeps the portal to Big Creative wide open, and the most amazing artists I know have it in spades. The willingness to get a glimpse of inspiration into form, even when it doesn't immediately make sense, is what separates the kick-ass creators from the plodding ones. Cultivate faith that Source is informing the work, and trust that your job is not to muscle it. Your job is not to pound and stretch and hammer disparate bits into submission and sense. Your job is to write it *down*. Get it into form. Allow your hands to piece things together. Good stewardship of inspiration is sometimes just getting the hell out of the way to let the Great Creator work through you.

Have you ever seen chefs in a kitchen when a knife falls out of their hands or gets bumped off a counter? They swiftly jump back out of the way. They're trained to do this early on so as not to make the mistake of trying to catch the knife or be stabbed in the foot by it. I'm not in the habit of thinking of creative inspiration as *falling knives*, per se, but inspiration does move fast and is worthy of our respect. When something shining and exact drops into your process, get out of the way and let it land.

Chapter Two: Big Creative

Who are the models of kick-ass creativity in your life? Are they members of your family or social circle? A contact in your profession?

1. List up to five people you admire, and after each of their names, note *why* you see them as so creativity potent.

____

____

____

____

____

2. When do you recall experiencing flow while growing up? Were there times when you remember a parent or teacher calling you "back to earth" because you were so engaged in an activity?

____

____

____

____

____

3. Down the left-hand column of a piece of paper, make a list of the activities or projects where you have recently experienced flow. Across the top of the paper, make column headings for "Location," "Time of Day," "Solo or with Whom," "Food/ Drink/Water, Rest," and "Other." For each occasion of flow, mark down what you recall about the elements around you. Note where patterns emerge, and integrate helpful elements into your sessions.

____

____

____

____

____

* **Bonus Kick-Ass Challenge:** Come up with a thirty-second "beckoning ritual" for invoking the experience of flow and an open, clear connection to Big Creative. Involve gesture, breath, candles, visualization, chakras—anything that speaks to you. Complete your ritual upon waking and before work sessions for the next seven days.

Opening the Flow

Project Rec: Make contact with one or two of your model creators and ask if you can schedule a conversation about creativity, whether a brief phone chat or meeting for a coffee or lunch. Share that you consider them a creative model and would like to know more about how they work. Most creative people will be flattered that you're interested in their journey and opinions. Write up ten or so questions in advance. Afterwards, adopt an element of their creative process (or try on their whole approach) as you work on your own pieces for the next few sessions. See how it feels and works for you, and integrate it into your own process accordingly.

Crazy-Easy Route: Focus your gaze on wherever you imagine Big Creative to physically reside (I like the big open expanse of sky, myself), and ask it to open on up for you the next time you'd like some help on a project. Be direct: "Yo! BC! I need a hand here, please!" Or be formal: "Dearest Big Creative, if you'd be so kind as to send down some lovely inspiration, please, I'd so appreciate it." Your approach doesn't matter. Just talk to the source of inspiration as if it's waiting for you to invite it into your process. (And know that some people insist that's *exactly* how it works.)

CHAPTER THREE

Focus and Vibrations

In order to really keep your energy makeover rocking, you've got to stock up your toolbox. You've got Big Creative and flow now happily tucked in your back pocket, but there are other great ways to keep creative energy rich and accessible.

The next several chapters will concentrate on energy amplifiers—tools that will help unlock our inner kick-ass creators by getting our energy strong and clear. These tools will help us dial in our desires, get high on our feelings, and learn to more effectively get the hell out of our own way. We'll start listening to ourselves, talking to ourselves, and opening up those rusty chakras. We'll tithe and writhe and move the furniture. Be warned: there will be work to do, changes to make, and ideas and strategies to implement with real commitment. There will be no whining. But there will be *focus.*

We'll start applying focus right away by paying more attention to where our attention and energy are going on a regular basis. We'll learn to consciously direct our focus toward only *the things, experiences, or feelings we want*, and see how focus naturally expands the energy around its targets. Then we'll amp up our energy even more with the fab four: desire, feelings, alignment, and allowing.

The Power of Focus

Focus matters in many contexts, but here we're going to concentrate on it as a way to define, direct, and expand our energy, all of which will aid us in our path to consistent, major contact with Big Creative. There has been a lot of interest in this particular kind of focus in the last few years, much of it helpful, but vague. We'll get specific and start applying it with other synergistic tools for most effective results. Let's start with the magnetic quality of focus, in the sense of *"like attracts like."*

Energy is sticky. It likes to clump together with other energy forms just like it. Think of it like a gaggle of girls in junior high—it prefers to move in clusters of parts that typically look, sound, and act the same. Energy's stickiness allows it to seek and gather similar energy nearby, at which point it grows and gets stronger (like junior high girls who've just found a mall!).

The concept of reflective, magnetic energy is well represented in religion and popular culture. It shows up in common sayings, like "What you sow, you reap," "Whatever you send out comes back to you," "What goes around, comes around," and "Water seeks its own level." It's pretty straightforward: *whatever you consciously experience leads to more of the same.*

We consider the repercussions of reflective—or returning—energy, in moments of social or moral awareness. We let someone in our lane during heavy traffic, thinking it's good to "do unto others as you'd have done to you." We inform the waiter of the missed items on our bill, just conscious of the possibility of "instant karma" coming back at us.

It's all related to the concept of magnetic, expansive energy: *like attracts like*.

Back in Chapter One's crash course in physics, we learned that human beings are made of vibrating energy. We're active, electromagnetic beings, absorbing and sending out energy messages all the time. All this energy bouncing around is like a highly charged magnet. The unique frequency of our personal energy—*our vibration*—seeks and attracts *similar frequencies* in every part of our lives. A *positive* focus connects us with Big Creative and attracts all the other bonuses of source energy; we vibrate high, fast, and happy, and find our lives full of good feelings. A *negative* focus brings low and slow vibrations, attracting more fear, frustration, self-consciousness, and other not-so-good feelings. Similar frequencies attract each other everywhere in our lives—in our relationships, resources, and the opportunities and problems that come our way.

Focus attracts opportunities for what we want to experience and feel.

Not quite sure if you buy the whole extending-of-our-energy-field/power-of-focus thing? Try this. The next time you're in a public place, choose a stranger whose back is turned to you and start staring at them. Say something to them in your mind, if you like—maybe, "Hey there, guy in the navy sweater." Watch how deliberately they turn around to see who is looking at them. You can get even more specific too, by staring at a specific body part. (Keep it clean, people.) Stare at the back of a stranger's head, a hand, or maybe shoulder and see if they don't twitch, reach up to touch the body part, or adjust their clothing, in a kind of response.[3] Focus and energy is real, and we can use it for much more important business than entertaining ourselves while in line at the post office.

When applied to our desires, focus attracts opportunities for what we want to experience and feel. It's like a flag to the universe, saying, "Here! This! This is what I want! Please send more right

3. For an in-depth examination of this phenomenon and other ways people and animals are connected energetically, see Rupert Sheldrake's fascinating book *The Sense of Being Stared At: And Other Unexplained Powers of the Human Mind* (New York: Three Rivers Press, 2004).

away!" Focus *defines*, *indicates*, and *expands* the energy around whatever what we want.

Bum bum *bum*—or whatever we *don't want*.

Both Sides of the Coin

Focus holds exceptional power because, like all our major energy tools, it swings both ways. Give attention to the essence of what you want, and you'll first *vibrate* the essence of what you want and then start *seeing* more of what you want; give attention to what you're worried about, angry over, or don't want, and you'll vibrate all that and see more of it show up in your life, to much dismay.

As much as the media or our "realist" friends might tell us it's important to prepare for the worst, we do better for ourselves to stay focused on the best in life: the love, the lightness, the accomplishments, the wisdom, the delights. When we *feel good*, we vibrate at the high levels closest to our original spiritual state. One of our most important tasks ahead will be learning to continually return to what *feels good*—to the *positive*—even when we'd love to defend our negativity.

Maybe there's a part of you asking: "Wait, is this just about 'positive thinking?' I've tried that. And it didn't get me everything I want." Yes, positive thinking is terrific, and important, but what we're embarking upon here is much deeper. We're looking beyond the benefits of positive pep talks, enthusiasm, and attitude; we're seeking to develop and maintain an enduringly positive *vibration.* Using focus to foster our highest vibrations allows us to pull our *best* selves out to play every time we decide to put raw, vulnerable ideas into form by the act of creating (even if what we're creating is just a cool life).

As with any powerful tool, there's temptation to want to claim all the benefits but also to conveniently believe the risks don't apply to us. If focusing and expanding lead to more money, great clients, fun opportunities, and beautiful work, we're all for it. "Go focus!

This rocks!" we say. However, if our focus drums up more anxiety, overdue bills, frustrating partners, or unexciting projects, we're ready to blame anything other than our mindset: "It's the economy." "It's my real job taking up too much time." "It's my spouse." But it's not. It's your focus, working overtime to pull in the fruits of your fears, worries, or complaints (exactly as effectively as it attracts good things when directed positively, by the way).

So how can we use focus to get our vibes in gear? We start by paying attention to where our focus goes on a regular basis (and making damn sure it's something we want to increase in our lives!). Researchers estimate that the average person thinks over sixty-five thousand thoughts a day, most of which are repetitive (and many of which are negative). Where is your current focus? If you were going to keep a "Thought Chronicle," logging every single thought you had in a day (an impossible, but intriguing proposition, I know), what would your major themes be? What's your primary emotional response to these themes? Your physical response? Do your current areas of focus generally energize and excite you? Do they worry, frustrate, or drain you? Make you angry or tight with anxiety? Do they not affect or move you much at all?

Managing our focus and feelings doesn't take genius, but it does take practice.

Thoughts indicate focus, but an even better way to become more conscious of focus and vibration is through the feedback of *feelings and emotions*. Managing our focus and feelings doesn't take genius, but it does take practice. So our next step is to take a closer look at feelings and how to work with them for our best energy and creativity.

Chapter Three: Focus and Vibrations

Let's look at where your attention is currently centered and how conscious you are about it. This can be an eye-opener.

1. What are your top five focus areas right now? These might be concerns, goals, points of excitement, or areas of attention where you notice yourself directing a lot of thought, feelings, emotion, or conversation.

2. How long has each focus area been prominent for you?

3. If you experienced the *exact outcome of your focus* in these five areas, what would you receive or feel? What would you be excited about? What are you worried might happen?

* **BONUS KICK-ASS CHALLENGE:** Are your focus areas similar to those of your partner, friends, or family members? Sometimes we vibrate in "tribes." Where do you crave change in your circle? Who do you know who might represent more exciting futures or possibilities? Could you reach out to them?

Opening the Flow

Project Rec: Take a focus inventory. Use a small voice recorder or notebook, and for a few hours, literally record the areas of your focus. If you're thinking/worrying/ wondering/excited/deliberating about something, it gets recorded. Find a creative way to remember to keep noting the results—a programmed cell-phone alert or the jangle of a rarely worn clothing item might help. This exercise can be ridiculously tricky, as our focus can move like lightning. Feel free to just put a star next to areas that come up more than once. At the end of your inventory period, sort your list into the three columns with these title headings: (1) Concerns/Worries, (2) Neutral/Chatter, and (3) Exciting/Positive. Put the most dominant topics at the top of each column. Carefully note any repetitive judgments you may have made on yourself or others.

Crazy-Easy Route: Call or email a close friend with whom you talk frequently, and ask *them* to list the five things that seem most prominent on *your* mind lately. Ask if the tone of these five topics represents a fairly typical outlook for you, or if it indicates a downward, steady, or upswinging trend. How does your friend's report compare with your own list from above? Is there a difference in how you present things to others and how you interpret them yourself?

CHAPTER FOUR

FEELINGS (WHOA, OH, OH . . .)

Artists feel deeply.

We're up. We're down. We're full of despair. We're on cloud nine. We're wounded. We're impenetrable. We're lost. We're certain.

We embody our feelings like nobody's business.

Our feelings have a way of guiding both the process and content of the work, sometimes unbeknownst to us. Upon reflection, our pieces divulge compelling evidence of our mental and emotional states—positive or negative—during their creation. We recognize the anguish in a series of paintings. The latest blogs reveal a growing pattern of hope and possibility. The sculpture shows our emerging feeling of power. The layouts are lifeless and flat. The latest photos show new intensity and purpose.

Although the archetype of the tortured artist remains part of popular culture, that doesn't mean we have to buy it.

Although the archetype of the tortured artist remains part of popular culture, that doesn't mean we have to buy it. We serve our work and ourselves better by releasing from negative identities and adopting the more productive, resilient, and exciting higher energy states of the *feel-good artist*. Let's start a movement now! It's time for us all to feel good, to feel *better*. Enough already with the gloom and doom! At the heart of it, aren't we having a good time? Feel-good artists enjoy the process of creating, because it's still as fun as it always was! We all know this: creating at a kick-ass, energized, brilliant level brings more fulfillment (and feels better!) than all the histrionic writhing we've done, deliciously dramatic and stimulating as it all may have been.

So we've got to find ways to *feel good*. Period. There's no room in our lives or our energy pipeline for the mess of trouble created by negative, sticky, crappy feelings. When we indulge in negativity—you know, the scorekeeping, irritation, hopelessness, anxiety, worries, jealousy, and pettiness—we close the door on other, more helpful forms of focus, and find ourselves drained of our potency, our power. It's easy to think that we're victims of our negative feelings, that they just *happen to us* spontaneously, but it's not true. We orchestrate our feelings with our choice of focus. The chain of events begins the moment we direct our attention and energy toward anything at all. Focus creates feelings, feelings create specific vibrations, and those vibrations create corresponding results in our lives—positive or negative. Feeling good energizes us and opens our valve to Big Creative. It's a no-brainer: we *must* find ways to consistently feel good.

I Think I'm Vibrating

Remember the last time you were terribly sad, and how depleted you felt? Or the time you were so angry that you were shaking, literally trembling with frustration? Or the time you were so thrilled that you felt like you were floating on air? Better than any other element in our lives, our feelings indicate how our inner energy is resonating.

Feelings and emotions work in close relationship to our thoughts, desires, and experiences, to serve as a barometer of *exactly how we're vibrating*. Whether they well up inside us or display themselves to the world in all their glory, emotions depict what's happening on our unique, personal energetic frequency. They tell the true vibrational story with tears, angry outbursts, or squeals of delight, especially when our big, busy brains try to convince us that we should appear cool, unbothered, together, or unimpressed.

Feelings and emotions help us interpret the other energy messages around us, too, as we constantly respond to the energy of the people, spaces, and objects around us. When we experience a mood shift in relation to a person or space, that's our feeling/emotional center helping us recognize that we've responded to a different energy. Babies and toddlers are pros at this kind of instant energy feedback. When they experience a change in energy, they let you know it; depending on the nature of the energy, kids will let out a massive wail, stop still in their tracks, or even start laughing.

Desire is our guide, and feelings are the unmistakable clues to help us find our way.

Our job in life is to experience happiness, and our paths to highest joy are marked by our individual desires. This is important, so I'll say it again in another way: *we want the particular things or experiences we do because they will lead us most directly to our deepest fulfillment.*[4] Desire is our guide, and feelings are the unmistakable clues to help us find our way.

Learning to recognize and direct our feelings and emotional energy will be one of the major ways we maximize our creative energy. Let's start by learning to *shift*.

The Gift of the Shift

You still can't find financial backers for your cool invention idea. Your partner is criticizing you all the time, and it's driving you nuts. You're way behind on your book proposal. You haven't had a good idea for a shoot in months. So what do you do?

4. This concept even inspired one of my songs a while back. It's called "Circle of Desire" and appears on my *Wish* album, (Musaic, 2005).

An instinctive tendency is to expand the negative thought or feeling into a full-fledged negative vibration. We corner our spouse or call a friend and go off in a tirade of complaining about the situation. We lie in bed at night and worry about it. We fret about the problem as we're driving. The more demonstrative among us (and by this, I do mean *me)* may even cry and mutter unproductive things to ourselves. We ruminate on things like "What am I going to do? How is this going to possibly work out? Why is this happening!?" and in the process, we add fuel to the negative fire.

We can usually catch ourselves before things get really serious, but occasionally, the urge to *wallow* is just too inviting. Yes, we know it's unproductive. Yes, we know it's exasperating and tiring to those around us. And yes, now we'll even worry that our negative vibes may sink us deeper into the crappola situation we're experiencing. Still we do it. Maybe we want a little attention, a little sympathy. Maybe it's our misguided way of seeking solutions. Or perhaps we're waiting for the deep organic shift that finally occurs when we've wallowed enduringly and loudly enough to begin annoying *ourselves* with our griping. And if you're even mildly self-aware, this moment *will* eventually occur. (I personally find that descending from an episode of too much coffee and an unrestrained carb binge brings my wallowing to a spectacular finale.) If you've been wallowing and finally do decide to emerge from your tight little cocoon of self-pity/irritation/disappointment, you'll break out either because you couldn't deal with your sad self any longer or because you're just ready for a *shift*.

Dozens of approaches can bring you to new, more empowered feelings, and they can help you far before things get really rough. The simplest way to change energy is to *shift our thoughts and focus to something better*. It doesn't need to be a grand gesture ("Major changing of the focus, here, please stand back!"). It can be as easy as switching to a new task, taking a break to get some fresh air, calling a friend to say hi, or making a cup of tea. The key is to find a way to seduce our attention away from whatever's bothering us.

Shifting can be as easy as changing your environment for a moment or disrupting the constrictive energy of a group. In songwriting sessions, there often comes a moment where the cowriters get stuck on a rhyme or lyric. I can't tell you how many times one writer will walk down the hall for a bathroom break or a soda and then burst back into the room with the perfect solution. It happens on a daily basis with our thoughts too. Haven't we all tried like crazy to remember a name or title, and then just when we'd forgotten all about it, had it pop into our heads?

When we shift our focus, we change our vibrational frequency so it can no longer build and grow on itself. An effective focus shift is like pressing the reset button on a piece of electronic equipment. We clean the slate of old residual information and have a fresh, new place to start. Most of us have built-in ways that we naturally shift, ways we've adopted over the years to manage stress. Workouts, food, sex, entertainment—we instinctively turn to these sensory stress-relievers not only for the physical and psychological rewards, but also because they allow us to find a more positive focus.

We've all heard it before: when we take care of ourselves, we have more to give.

Now that we know there are additional energetic benefits, we can expand our shifting repertoire with even more gusto! The following are a few cool ways of shifting focus that have proven to be especially effective for us delightfully sensory artistic types.

The Self-Care Shift

Start your shift process with some self-care. We all work hard to take care of our families, associates, friends, and even pets; it can feel like the demands on us never end. Remembering to take care of ourselves—and finding the time and support to make it happen—can become a low-priority item in our busy lives. Instead, ridiculously, our initial instinct can be to try to *do even more.* "Maybe if I woke up an hour earlier, I could manage better," we imagine. "I should work harder," we think. "I should get more disciplined." Here's where our puritanical roots start showing. Of course there's a place for hard work and discipline, but when we're exhausted or chronically annoyed, instituting demanding new structures is not the answer. We've all heard it before: when we take care of ourselves, we have more to give. We replenish our spiritual and creative wells by listening to ourselves.

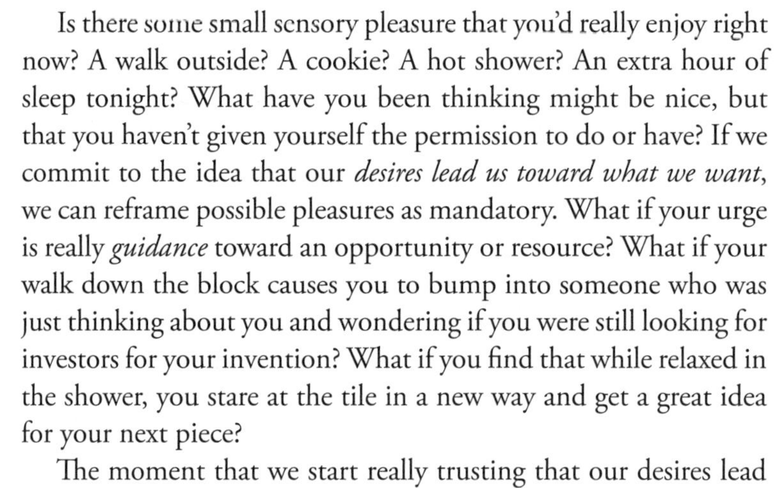

Is there some small sensory pleasure that you'd really enjoy right now? A walk outside? A cookie? A hot shower? An extra hour of sleep tonight? What have you been thinking might be nice, but that you haven't given yourself the permission to do or have? If we commit to the idea that our *desires lead us toward what we want*, we can reframe possible pleasures as mandatory. What if your urge is really *guidance* toward an opportunity or resource? What if your walk down the block causes you to bump into someone who was just thinking about you and wondering if you were still looking for investors for your invention? What if you find that while relaxed in the shower, you stare at the tile in a new way and get a great idea for your next piece?

The moment that we start really trusting that our desires lead us toward good things, *good things start happening*.

The moment that we start really trusting that our desires lead us toward good things, *good things start happening.*

For several months last year, I worked excitedly on a new project: a deck of intuition cards for artists. It started as a private set of cards for myself, to use when I felt blocked or frustrated, but it quickly grew into something I felt others might find helpful too.

It started out like gangbusters. I was flowing like crazy, staying up late, writing on scraps of paper during lunch, inspired and energized about all the ways this endeavor might be of service to my artist friends and creative folks around the world.

But as the deck got close to being finished, I found myself full of resistance. I felt deflated, cranky, exhausted, certain that with my current responsibilities (and an eight-month-old baby!), there would never enough time to work out and complete everything I wanted to do with the cards. "Maybe it was a stupid idea," I thought. "Maybe I'm not the one to make these. There's probably something like this already out there anyway." I trawled the murky depths of the *what ifs* and the *oh wells*. (Imagine the irony—*I* certainly see it; I was blocked on a project to help those who are blocked!)

It wasn't until I was able to *shift my focus* that things began to change and lighten up. I didn't shift into a forced, high-action mode of doing, doing, and oh yes, some more *doing*, though the industrious little worker bee in me wondered if that was the answer. Instead, I stopped everything. I asked myself what I'd been *really craving* that I'd resisted giving myself, what specific kind of self-care I'd been neglecting. Instead of five uninterrupted hours to work, did I really just want a *nap*? A massage? To enjoy a glass of wine with a friend? If our desires are indeed a roadmap for reaching our dreams, I'd gone *way* off course. By ignoring my instincts and desires, I'd been metaphorically crumpling up my map and throwing it out the window. I'd been driving hard and fast, all right—in the *wrong direction*.

I needed to center myself in the midst of all the daily chaos, to find a way to *feel good* in some way, *any* way, and then maybe I'd be able to recall the part of me that might have something to offer the creative community. Then, perhaps, I could access some inspiration and excitement and vision again.

I directed my efforts toward arranging an afternoon off from my usual life. I got my ragged nails done (a luxury for this new mom), browsed at a bookstore, caught up with a friend over a chai, and had a great time shopping for an hour in a gourmet food store. It was astonishing. Suddenly I felt more like myself again. I was ready to write, ready to move forward, ready to again journey down the path that just hours before had felt so daunting. Chunks of available time seemed to open up magically in my weekly schedule. Everything became more possible. I began writing again, furiously, with inspired words flowing out freely and beautifully about how to release stubborn blocks and loosen ourselves from resistance and inertia. It felt wonderful. I think of the products of those writing sessions as the "manicure manifesto."

Don't Do Anything, Just Sit There

Another effective way to shift out of an unproductive focus and into something better is to just let go. Our addiction to constant *doing and analyzing and thinking* can be tough to break, but there's a kind of universal autopilot that serves us incredibly well when the skies get really choppy. We activate this autopilot mode by simply

taking our hands off the rudder. We breathe. We repeat a calming mantra, such as, "Everything is unfolding in perfect order, for my highest good." We let go of the need to feel as if we're in control, and we find relief and clarity in the stillness, the silence.

When yoga started gaining popularity awhile back, I jumped on the bandwagon. With gusto I began heading off to group classes, doing herbal cleanses, and meditating—sitting on my mat every morning, observing my breath. Although I didn't stick with the yoga classes—my wrists always hurt and I only seemed to really get into *savasana*, the part at the end where you kind of take a little rest—I did decide to stay with the meditation practice until I'd given it a committed try. I thought it might create a shortcut to some kind of guidance or divine wisdom for me, or that it might be able to calm down my task-obsessed brain. In any case, with so much noise and media around these days, it seemed like a good idea to just find some quiet. And it was. It helped. After sitting, I would feel less overwhelmed, less freaked out, and more trusting that everything was happening with a sense of positive purpose. I felt better afterwards than I did before I meditated, and the time it took up seemed to easily deposit itself back into my schedule throughout the day.

I accepted that meditation was working, but I didn't really know why. Why would just sitting there, relaxing and breathing (in . . . and out, in . . . and out) make one dang bit of difference in my life? Was I really, really tired and getting micronaps somehow? Was I so overloaded and mentally knotted up that just those few minutes of detangling my brain every day was somehow helping everything run more smoothly?

I finally came to a conclusion that made sense. When I sit in silence, I find myself almost automatically loosening and releasing any sticky, negative energy I might have gathered around me. Esther and Jerry Hicks, in the Abraham book *Ask and It Is Given*, explain that sometimes we become like corks pulled deeply underwater, where the pressure is uncomfortable and movement is slow. When we meditate, we *let go* of the day-to-day details that keep us tethered to lower energies and find ourselves popping up to the surface of higher energies. It's like our spirits are renewed, saying, "Ah, yes, floating along happily again. No need to worry, stress, or force anything. That's right, just floating downstream delightfully toward everything I've ever wanted. Much, much better."

When you need to stop doing, doing, doing—and you *know* when you need to—just let go. Shut everything off, set a mellow alarm, sit or lay down with your spine nice and straight, and breathe in and out for ten minutes. You might feel that you're supposed to be *doing* something to get the best results, but *you're not.* Surrender to the idea that all you need to do is breathe; all you need to do is keep returning your awareness to the fact that "Oh, I'm breathing in, and now I'm breathing out." Don't worry if your mind tries to keep rolling at a breakneck pace; there's no prize for being the best meditator. (Well, maybe there is in monk school, or something, but not here.) It's just about slowing down, narrowing your focus to your breath, and letting everything else (including resistance, worry, and negativity) drift away for a few minutes, leaving you clear and ready to look at things in a new way.

When you need to stop doing, doing, doing—and you *know* when you need to—just let go.

Forgettaboutit!

What about when something really awful happens, and you get really worked up? Here's a wild approach: just *forget it.* Stop worrying about it, thinking about it, analyzing it, wondering this or that about it. Yep, you heard me. Shift your *assets* out of the situation by doing something completely different, something that makes you feel good, at ease, and normal.

It may sound over-simplistic, but forgetting about whatever's gotten you hoppin' mad can be a huge help to an overwhelmed psyche. Sometimes we're not ready to look at a situation with an objective eye and figure what the most beneficial next step might be, where our part of the responsibility lies, or how we can work toward a solution. Sometimes all we feel capable of is stepping away from frustrating circumstances for a while. This space can be enough, as it allows us to clear some of the negative vibes away.

It's kind of like cleaning the basement. You may know there's a lot of work ahead—sure, you're going to eventually paint and

bring in fabulous new furniture—but for the moment, clearing out the cobwebs, junk, and dust is making a huge difference in how it looks and feels. By finding something to do that takes you out of a maddening setting (or mindset), you clear out the mental garbage you're frantically rearranging in your head, and you welcome some new light on the issue. Doing so will lead you to a better position from which to later reassess the situation.

Here's a story illustrating how well the "forget it" approach can work: My friend Andrew recently got worked up about a disputed writing credit for a screenplay he'd cowritten. The film began getting hyped for its premiere, and the credit issue was still unresolved. Andrew panicked. What if no one believed that he'd been a cowriter? What if this were the only screenplay of his to make it into theaters, and his name wasn't even on it? What if his former partners made tons of money, and he was still struggling in his ugly awful apartment with his decrepit laptop? It wasn't fair!

All the parties involved knew that Andrew deserved some of the credit and profits from the project, but there seemed to be an impasse. No one was taking his calls, he'd received a scary cease-and-desist letter, and it looked like he'd have to find a way to go after his co-writers *and* the studio now, with their big shot expensive lawyers. Not good.

The night of the premiere came, and Andrew made plans to go. He wanted to experience the thrill of seeing his film on the big screen for the first time. Another part of him wanted to go just to look the other writers right in the eye and show them he wasn't afraid or intimidated (even though he was).

However, when a friend suggested they do something else instead, something ridiculous and fun, he accepted, deciding to forget the (expletive omitted) film premiere. He and his friend went surfing, something Andrew hadn't allowed himself the time to do in months. They paddled out on a beautiful L.A. evening and began to ride the waves toward shore. Suddenly, nothing else mattered except catching the next shoulder and keeping steady on the board. At one point, the sky was so beautiful that the two surfers sat on their boards and watched the sunset.

Andrew joked, "Wouldn't it be funny if the guys were thanking me right now for my invaluable contributions to the film? 'Oh, Andrew, are you here?'" he shouted with a flourish, "'cause we couldn't have done it *without you*!" He and his friend laughed and paddled back out, riding the surf until they were fabulously exhausted and famished.

The next day, Andrew received a call from his writing partners' attorney. "We'd like to get this matter settled right away," the lawyer said. "I hope the recognition last night assures you that we're interested in an amicable resolution here." Andrew pressed for more details. "What recognition?" he asked. "Oh, weren't you there?" the lawyer said, surprised. "The guys made a point to thank you for your part in revising the script and apologized that you'd been omitted from the credits."

Andrew was flabbergasted. It didn't even make sense! Why in the world would they change tack so suddenly now? And then he thought back to the joke while surfing. He'd been completely at ease while out on the water—confident, powerful. If anything, for the first time in ages, he felt free and unworried about whatever might happen with the film and his credit. And at the *exact* moment that he was joking about receiving his recognition, it was being given to him at the premiere!

Andrew attributes the shift in his writing partners' behavior to his own shift that evening out on the water. The instantaneous, astonishing change in the situation had to be related to *something*. Andrew decided it must have been the energy.

Smile Therapy

Feelings affect our bodily systems in specific, measurable ways. We usually see this as a one-way action: if we feel a certain way (say, anxious or scared), our bodies respond physically in a predictable manner (with an increased heart rate, blood pressure, and a little sweat, maybe). What many of us don't consider, however, is that this response works inversely as well. The physical actions of our bodies also affect our feelings. And it doesn't take a full-on workout

When we smile, synapses start firing all over the place, like little search engines seeking the reason for this sudden smiling.

to stimulate endorphins and better feelings—even subtle gestures or actions can make a difference in our vibrations.

Take smiling, for instance. When we smile, a series of neurotransmitters releases in our brains, setting off a chain reaction of pleasurable hormone changes and physical responses. Synapses start firing all over the place, like little search engines seeking the reason for this sudden smiling. Our *feelings* start changing in response to a simple physical act.

For an exceptionally energizing shift, try finding a quiet spot where you won't be disturbed (or be worried that you'll look like an idiot). Then close your eyes, think of something that makes you feel calm and happy, and allow a soft, warm smile to come across your face. (By the way, if you can't think of a smile-worthy thought to get you started, just go ahead and smile anyway and see where it leads you.) You're going for the kind of tender, gentle smile you might have while holding an infant, or while relaxing after a hard, rewarding hike, or while savoring something warm and delicious, like a piece of hot, buttery bread. Let your smile melt across your whole face and then move down your neck and shoulders, down your back, until it fills your body with a loving, happy feeling. Umm! Yeah, that's it. Doesn't that feel great?

In her memoir *Eat, Pray, Love,*[5] Elizabeth Gilbert is instructed by her spiritual teacher to meditate by smiling. "Smile with your whole body," the teacher advised. "Smile with your liver." Exactly! When we start smiling with our whole selves—our bodies, our cells—something amazing happens. We instantly lighten and lift. We expand energetically. Our problems diminish in size and power, and we *feel better*, setting the stage for better things to come into our lives.

Historically Effective Shifts

It's hard to pinpoint what exact path leads us to an off-kilter feeling sometimes. "Why am I so tired or negative?" I'll wonder in an

5. Gilbert, Elizabeth. *Eat, Pray, Love: One Woman's Search for Everything Across Italy, India, and Indonesia.* New York: Viking, 2006.

off moment. Is it my horoscope? Something someone said? Just an occasional part of being the parent of a two-year-old? I get very hypochondriacal in my lesser moments. Could it be a B-vitamin deficiency? Too little sleep? Too much sleep? Seasonal affective disorder? I've heard a lot about underactive thyroids lately. Oh, and *gluten!* Maybe it's the gluten!

It could be one of these things. Or it could be I've gotten sucked into a negative focus, and I just need try one of my proven shifts—an activity that I know puts me in a better energetic place. Try it. Creating a collection of historically effective shifts for you to reference in tough moments can help you sidestep the bad-attitude fairy that tries to dissuade you from trying anything.

Make a list of your favorite shifts and post it somewhere that's easily accessible, like the inside of a cupboard. Or write them down on pieces of paper and put them in a mug to pick from when you need some guidance. Or draw or paint them on big, pretty marbles with a Sharpie or nail polish, and place them in a cool jar on your windowsill to shiningly remind you that you can reach in anytime and grab an idea for a fun, light thing you'll enjoy doing.

My list looks like this:

Want to feel better?

Hang out with Mark (my husband) on the deck

Watch a cooking show or bake something

Write in my journal

Drink some water

Tidy up something that's bugging me

Play with Daisy (our toddler daughter)

Lie down for a nap

Take some fish oil and cal/mag/zinc

Play computer Scrabble

Meditate

Take a bath

Call Jill

Go for walk in the forest

Your list should be delightfully unique, like *you*. Just give yourself a way to access to your shifts that doesn't require you to trawl your entire brain for something that sounds positive when you're feeling crummy. The snarky voice of "It probably won't work" is much less convincing when you can just look at, grab, or roll out a happy option.

As you embark upon the journey of attracting your deepest, most thrilling levels of creativity and all its fun, related desires, I encourage you to begin with what simply feels *good*. This, paradoxically, is often best defined by what does *not* feel good. In the next chapter, we explore how to unwrap our desires from the tricky, sticky disguises they occasionally use.

Chapter Four: Feelings (Whoa, Oh, Oh...)

Feelings do a superb job of giving us immediate feedback on our current focus and vibration. What are your feelings and emotions uncovering for you lately?

1. Describe or represent the tone of your *ideal life* using three words, sounds, colors, or images. Now show the tone of

your *current life* using three such elements. Where is there alignment? Contrast?

2. What are the three dominant feelings you've been experiencing daily lately? Do these feelings support the expansion of your ideal or current life?

3. Make a list of ten pleasurable activities or mental escapes that might serve as effective shifting techniques for you. How often do you use these techniques already? Which do you find most effective?

* **Bonus Kick-Ass Challenge:** Got a tenacious negative focus? Have a Smile Intervention Session. Set aside ten minutes when you won't be disturbed, hold the concern in your mind, and open yourself up to help. Imagine your concern surrounded by a warm pink light. Then start smiling. Allow your concern to float up to Big Creative, where it can be resolved quickly and easily. After your meditation, whenever your concern comes to mind, remind yourself that inspiration, aid, and resolution are on the way.

Opening the Flow

Project Rec: Embark on a Daylong Feeling Diary. On the hour, or more often if you wish, use lines, squiggles, and/or circles to create a visual record of your feelings throughout the day. Log them on any surface you want (sketch pad, magazine, newspaper, clay) with any instrument you like (crayon, pen, marker, utility knife). Allow your marks to spiral, go off the page, or whatever—they need not be linear. Note how they change in pressure and movement throughout the day. (Analytical types: feel free to chart your feelings on a vertical scale from 1 [hopeless, freaked out] to 10 [thrilled, joyful].) When you sense a strong change in your feelings (and thus your vibration), take a moment to note your trigger; try to pinpoint the specific action, activity, thought, or words that brought about the change. These are some of your default shifts, for better or worse. Need to shift? Try one of the ideas in this chapter, or draw from your own faithful collection.

Crazy-Easy Route: Go get yourself a cookie. You heard me. Right now. And by cookie, I don't mean only a delectable baked treat, but any small thing that would feel like a treat. It can be short and sweet—a quick snuggle or moment of sunshine counts, too. Go on—just go get it or do it.

CHAPTER FIVE
DESIRE

WHAT YOU REALLY, REALLY WANT

Artists desire.

We're a thirsty bunch, glad to readily drink of life's pleasures—the sensory delights, the thrill of connection, the witness of transformation, the buzz of energy. We seek comfort, rapport, inspiration, resources, rewards. The creative road can challenge one's self-worth, leading many of us to desire specific facets of positive feedback, such as recognition, affirmation, and validation.

Artists are sometimes discouraged from cultivating desire. The art should be enough, we're told. We shouldn't want for material things. We shouldn't crave fame or fortune or awards. After all, we're lucky enough to be creating! We're blessed vessels for inspiration! Our satisfaction derives from the work, the process. *The art should be enough.*

Bullshit.

Once we know what we'd like to *feel*, we find a way for the desire to be represented by a person, place, thing, or experience.

Artists *must* work with desire, all kinds of desire, to do what we're here to do. *Desire guides us to our deepest purpose in life.* Without it, we're adrift without a compass. Following one's bliss isn't always popular or advocated—deprivation of one sort or another frequently comes into fashion—but it's essential for artists. We honor our spiritual path by knowing what we want and creating it in our lives.

Moreover, desire traffics in feelings, and artists (as you know) *love* feelings. I think our constant contact with energy makes us emotional-stimulation junkies. We endure the ups and downs, fearlessly engaging with dramatic lows and thrilling highs, as the last chapter discussed. We get burned when we're not careful, but we're happy to be deep in a tangle of feelings most of the time. They're just too delicious!

Besides, we're not really materialistic. Our wants merely represent the desire for a specific *feeling*. A desire for lots of money might represent a yearning for freedom, security, or options. That guitar we want? Maybe it turns us on because we imagine we'll feel more skilled, talented, or admired when we play it. Our lives are full of simple equations of desire and feelings. "If I have *this*, I'll feel *that*," we instinctively sense. Desire settles in around a feeling and then takes form in our lives. Once we know what we'd like to *feel*, we find a way for the desire to be represented by a person, place, thing, or experience. This dance of feelings and desire happens instantaneously and subconsciously. It takes only an instant to decide that something, someone, or someplace *just might make you feel better* than you do at a given moment. In that instant, a new desire is born.

Wanting, Wanting, and More Wanting

Desires appear in our lives in positive, negative, and disguised forms.

A *positive desire* might show up as an affirmative hope (or intention) for a specific thing or experience, such as "I want to have a show at that great new gallery" or "I want to get together with that total hottie from the glassblowing studio." Positive desires serve as the gold standard. They're clean, clear, and ready for all the energy you can invest in them.

A *negative desire* emerges first in the form of a complaint, but can be easily turned around to reflect a positive side. "My partner doesn't support me," we say, when we really mean, "I'd love my partner to be excited and supportive of my work." "There's no money in photography anymore," we say, actually meaning, "I want to find a market that appreciates and pays a fair rate for my photography." In order to get negative desires working for us, we first need to do this quickie little conversion process, called *flipping*.

Lastly, there are *disguised desires*. These are kind of tricky—they can look like positive desires, but are actually based on avoidance or lack. "I want to get out of debt," we say, but the message is, "I don't want to be in debt." A better way to state the desire might be: "I want to have plenty of money for everything I need." An easy way to recognize a disguised desire is to see if the desire gets you *out* of a negative situation instead of *into* an exciting one. Move toward the desire, not just vaguely away from what's not working. *Toward the desire.*

What's the Flippin' Issue?

I'm going to go out on a limb here and guess that you don't have everything you want.

If you're not happy with your work or your life at the moment, what's going on? What exactly is getting you down? Is it about money? Balance? Time? Support? Validation? Image? Freedom? Skills?

Let's try something. I don't recommend this as a frequent exercise (because it happens occasionally for most of us without incentive), but take a moment to just go ahead and complain. That's right, bitch it up. Surrender to the urge and let it fly. You can even

Our job is to identify what we are *actually seeking* to be, have, or do, not to pinpoint all the situations and experiences we'd rather avoid.

use unproductive language and profanity if you like, just for some good gusto in the presentation.

Maybe you're angry: "Nobody ever *!%#* supports me!" "Those #&%!# bigwigs never recognize real talent like mine!" "How come that #%&! jerk gets all the cushy jobs!" Or you may prefer more of a mopey, resigned mode: "No one understands the level of what I'm trying to do." "I never get selected for _____." "Nothing ever changes in the lame scene here." You might choose to go with a litany of *I can'ts*, as in "I can't get a break" or "I can't ever find enough time." You may find yourself similarly having fun and resonance with the ever-popular "It's not my fault, it's my ____" theme (insert *family, debt, background, job, town,* or whatever else you wish here).

Do I sound unsympathetic? I'm not. I've had enough pissed-off muttering-to-myself conversations in my car to make it across the country and back. I'm just being lighthearted about it, because I've learned to trust that no experience is set in stone. You have the power to easily change anything you don't like. We all take on disempowered roles at times in our lives. We've all been the victim, underdog, misunderstood intellectual, low man, failure, or fallen hero, at least for a short while. What matters is not that we visit this sketchy terrain; what matters is that we use the information we get there to help us identify what we'd prefer to experience instead. Our job is to identify what we are *actually seeking* to be, have, or do, not to pinpoint all the situations and experiences we'd rather avoid.

We transform and empower our unproductive energy by *flipping* complaints or disguised negative wants into positive desires. Sometimes there's a clear inverse, other times you may need to be more creative about wording or interpretation to make your "don't want" into something you do want.

To flip, we state the facts of our desired state-of-being as authoritatively as we do our complaints. Be specific. Be authoritative. Make it feel possible (it can be a *stretch*, but must still feel *possible.*) Write it down to make the whole process feel more official, if you like. You might choose to do it affirmation style, where you make a statement of *being*, rather than a statement of want. Put it in the present tense. State it as if it's already in motion for you. To flip the first three examples, we might say "I experience wonderful support" (instead of "No one ever supports me") or "Imaginative, influential bigwigs are discovering and appreciating my work more every day" (instead of "Those idiot bigwigs never recognize real talent like mine!"). Try something like, "People tell me all the time how inspired they are by the depth and courage of my work" (instead of "No one understands the level of what I'm trying to do"). Noticing what you *don't want* allows a clear picture of what you *do want* to come to the surface almost effortlessly.

Our frustrations might get us down sometimes, but at least they can shed some light on what's really going on, where our desire really lies. Perhaps this is the universe's quiet offering in our hours of dissatisfaction, the little sparkle in the fields at rest. If it's true that there's a gift in everything, the gift of whining must bring the opportunity for clarity.

The Roads to Desire

How do we *usually* go about getting something we want? For many things, we can go the old-fashioned way and earn them through hard work and perseverance, of course. We can also ask (or hint for) someone else to provide our desire. If we want a high position or big job, we can make a master plan, and then break it down into small, manageable steps that will ostensibly bring us to our goal. We can use our resources to find a creative way to borrow or trade it. We can even steal it (though that's not typically recommended among us karmically aware types).

What if we want something less tangible, more emotional and internal? Tried and true acquisition methods guarantee little success for finding love, personal satisfaction, career fulfillment, and harmonious families, for instance. At best, applying traditional approaches to these more elusive desires feels like overkill—and at worst, it's a frustrating waste of time and effort.

Instead, we instinctively turn to *energy* to help us attract what we want. Most of us sense that some of our wants require special treatment, so we institute energetic practices ranging from subtle, simple forms of hope to more demonstrative, structured daily rituals. Do be assured that *all* people—not just us creators or new-agey folk—rely on energetic approaches when seeking certain desires, by the way, whether they realize it or not; it's as if human beings intuitively know that some lovely things in life must be sought in special ways. Those less certain about energy work may deny that there is an energetic component (or personal vibrational contribution) to life's twists and turns, but revealingly, folks in this camp frequently acknowledge a divine order through comments such as "What happens, happens," "It just wasn't meant to be," or "She (or he) just wasn't the one."

Priming the Pump

People use all kinds of energetic approaches to magnetizing their desires. Some people write down their goals and desires in lists or journals. The more visually inclined might make a vision collage or dream board, or they might spend time mentally visualizing what their goals would look like if they come true. Others might do daily affirmations, come up with dream scenarios, or participate in workshops or self-discovery projects. These paths help define our desires. They're also fun, creative, and centering. So why don't they work?

Okay, to be fair, I should ask: how could they work better, faster, and more consistently?

It comes back to feelings. I don't mean to belabor the point, but it's critical: feelings pave the way for anything we want to be, do, or have. In book 3 of Neale Donald Walsch's *Conversations With God* series,[6] he addresses something called the be-do-have paradigm. Here's the gist: most of us believe that if we *have* the things we

6. Walsch, Neale Donald. *Conversations With God: An Uncommon Dialogue (Book 3).* Charlottesville, VA: Hampton Roads Publishing Company, 1996

want, we'll get to *do* the things we want, and then we'll become the person we want to *be*. But we have it backwards. It's by *being* who we want to be (feeling like we want to feel) that we discover what to *do* in order to acquire what we'd like to *have*.

It might go something like this: we might think, "If I had lots of money and time, I'd paint all the time and be content and relaxed." In reality, there's no need to wait. We can find the part of ourselves that already feels (knows!) how to be content and relaxed, which can lead to painting for fun and recreation, which can lead to an awareness of plentiful time and resources (or even potential buyers or patrons of our work, whose support would allow us to paint even more).

Play the "and then what" game. Name a desire, and then ask yourself what it would mean to you in terms of what would happen next.

In this context, being means *feeling* with our whole, fabulous selves. We activate the strongest, swiftest, most powerful, most advantageous energy in the universe on behalf of little ol' us the moment we embody the *feeling*—the essence—of our desired outcome. The process of consciously getting into the feeling state of what you want is called *scripting*. We script by using as many of our senses and imaginative talents as we can muster, in order to, well, *activate the vibration* of the feelings we want.

When done well, affirmations, lists, and other tools can help us find the strong "feeling place" of our desires, but it's the *feeling* that's the key, not the affirmations, lists, or tools themselves. We can visualize, make collages, chant, and write until the cows come home, but, again, if no *feelings* are cultivated, we won't see even a *blip* of that desire on the horizon. It's not the specific actions we do that bring in our desires, it's the *feelings* we drum up with those actions or scripts that really matter.

How do we know what feeling is at the heart of our desires? We can get to the feeling cores of our desires by playing the "and then what" game. Name a desire, and then ask yourself what it would mean to you in terms of what would happen next. It usually takes fewer than five questions to get to the essence of a desire.

For instance, say my desire is that I want to win a Pulitzer Prize. "If I won my Pulitzer," I might ask myself, "then what?" That would probably mean a lot of people knew and liked my work.

If tons of people were appreciating my writing, then what? That means I might get to do fun stuff, like go to dinners with interesting public figures and be interviewed on national talk shows. Okay, if I'm enjoying statusy dinners and being interviewed on big talk shows, then what? That means I'm probably acknowledged to be a person with talent, skills, and insight. And what would that kind of recognition mean to me? That I'm successful and respected. And then what might being successful and respected mean for me? It might mean that I desire to *matter*. I want to contribute something of value, and to experience the feeling of being *valued*.

Years ago, my roommate Kendall and I played the "and then what" game one night as she tried to figure out what to do next with her twenty-something life. Her desires started with wanting lots of money, but the end-point desire was actually to use her time and resources to help people. It was empowering to discover that she could, in fact, choose to *skip* the daunting "how can I build a massive fortune?" conundrum, and instead move right to the "helping people" phase. Unearthing the true essence of our surface desires can always help when we feel powerless or uncertain of where to direct our efforts.

Once More, With Feeling

I spent years—okay, a decade—thinking that if I only practiced harder, was more talented, became more attractive, networked better, or read more books, I'd get what I wanted from my music. I learned a lot during those years—don't get me wrong—but mostly I ended up feeling like I had worked a lot harder than many of my peers for less exciting results.

Things only started changing for me when I started embracing the idea of *really feeling what I wanted.* I began believing in the actual possibility of my dreams in a visceral way. I started using my imagination and ingenuity to create a new script—to completely immerse myself in the feelings I hoped to experience from my desires (a better gig, better music income, my songs on TV shows). The very moment I started embodying the feeling of what I wanted, I started having much more success at seeing it show up in my life.

I started out by doing what *felt good* to me, no matter how ridiculous it might have appeared to anyone else. I wrote in my journal about the fun things "already happening" to me. I talked to myself, frequently having conversations with my idols I was "now" working with. I made up and sang happy little songs to myself about the fun gigs I had and all the perks that came along with them. (I'm sure a reality show would've had a heyday with me, but who cares! I was creating, dammit!)

And I daydreamed—*boy, did I daydream.* I created fabulous scenarios, imagining myself standing at the post office, opening my mail to see a check for tens of thousands of dollars, feeling the rush of excitement and possibility that the money would bring. I directed all available energy toward *feeling* the *feeling* of my desire with every ounce of my being, utilizing many of the same tools I use as a songwriter to put me into the right place: imagination, detail specificity, sensory references, metaphors, emotion.

And it worked! It was so cool!

When I decided I wanted to amp up my performance opportunities awhile back, I thought a big outdoor concert might be fun. So I started regularly imagining a fantastic performance, right down to the shoes I was wearing. I saw it in my mind often enough that soon I could *feel* myself walking off the stage, *feel* my heart beating with excitement, *feel* the thrill after the set had gone so well and *feel* the audience's enthusiastic response. I could *feel* the huge smile on my face as I saw the line form for people wanting to purchase my CDs, *feel* the hugs from my great friends and audience members who had been moved by the music. There was an almost carbonated feeling rush in my stomach as I experienced this "future moment" so realistically. I even started preparing as if the concert were coming up. I started thinking about a set list, working out more regularly, scheduling a few extra rehearsals with the band, and keeping an eye out for an outfit with a perfect little sparkle in it.

A wonderful opportunity came up just weeks later, when I got a call to open for the legendary Etta James in front of thousands at a massive outdoor concert venue. The crowd was amazing, I felt great about the set, and I ended up selling hundreds of records at the show that night (something which rarely happens for opening acts). I found myself feeling a sense of déjà vu; because I'd already felt the performance so fully and realistically in my mind and body, the actual experience seemed like a flashback. Wild—and lovely.

Finale Thinking

When we know what our desired ending is, the universe can begin flowing in to fill the blanks.

Performers know that in the moments after a spectacular finale, we take our final bow, and our senses fill with the sights and sounds around us. We're released from the structure of the song, movement, words, or story we'd committed to share, and we can freely open to the visceral world around us. We hear the audience applaud, we see the lights dim, we feel the curtains brush against us as they close. We're filled with a sense of relief, delight, and gratitude that another show has gone so well.

This is the *exact moment* I want you to imagine as you choose a feeling state to embody when drawing your desires into your life. When we know what our desired ending is, the universe can begin flowing in to fill the blanks. So go ahead—put yourself in the moment just after the grand finale. You need not worry about how your show—in whatever form it might appear—will be mounted, funded, or staged. You need not worry about who the other players are, whether it's been a long or short run, or if you've been singled out for special recognition or criticism. Your only task is to find the moment of relief, delight, and gratitude at *the conclusion of your desired experience*.

Of all the positive feelings out there, why hone in on relief, delight, and gratitude? Why work with these three elements in particular?

When we cultivate *relief*, we cover our bases. It must have gone well, or you wouldn't feel relieved. You must have *stretched* a bit, or you wouldn't have felt the tension of worry or nervousness. You must have felt the full engagement of *flow*, your best effort, or you wouldn't be so glad it worked out after all.

When we cultivate *delight*, we ensure our enjoyment. What's the fun of a desire that ends up being more stressful and full of hassles than you ever expected? Delight signifies unexpected pleasures and gifts. When we feel delight, we are surprised with the level of our joy. We've exceeded even our own expectations.

And when we cultivate *gratitude*, our individual spirits expand. We reconnect with Big Creative and return energy to the grand current. We lift from the minutiae of the moment and sense the scope of this experience in the greater perspective of our lives. We mark it in our memories. Our vibration shimmers with clarity and power.

Finale thinking can be applied at several stages of the creative process. Use it anytime you need a lift. It can help with the completion phase of a piece, with preparations for presentation, or even to pave the way for positive reviews or future career opportunities.

For instance, if you're a writer in the middle of a project, you might start by cultivating the feeling of what you'll experience as you write the final sentence of your piece, the huge sense of relief, excitement, pride, and thanks as you finish those last perfect words. Then you might work on defining and embodying the finale moment for other parts of the process. Get into the feeling-place of your fantastic book-signing or release party, where people are excitedly shaking your hand and asking you to write specific dedications on the several hard-cover copies that they just purchased. Write some glowing reviews for yourself—exactly the kind of things that would make you feel understood and validated and successful if you were to see them in print. Imagine that you're talking with your thrilled agent (this can be someone you don't know yet, by the way), who has amazing news about the play you just finished or the big Hollywood studio that wants to buy the film rights to your novel.

Have fun with it! Take your bow and clutch those gorgeous roses. Enjoy your *finale*.

Skip to a part of your piece that's *fun*, even if it's not the next step chronologically.

And Then Have Even More Fun

Another way to get into the feeling place of something you want is to integrate it into the rhythm of your current project. Skip to a part of your piece that sounds like *fun* (because remember, that's inspiration talking), even if it's not the next step chronologically or something that makes particularly logical sense. It can even be part of the piece or process in which you won't realistically participate, such as reviewing your own show.

Try anything that sounds fun (and would be exciting in "real" life). Write out your thank-you page or speech, and ride the grateful vibe you create as you recall all the kind and generous people who make your projects possible. Fool around with the title in different fonts and layouts, or make up imaginary promotional blurbs from hugely influential bigwigs. "Transcribe" that brilliant interview you gave on a national talk show (that just hasn't happened to take place yet).

It can also be helpful (and a nice change of pace) to jump to a part of the project that involves a different art form. If you work in words, play with images for a while. Noodle around with cover or poster ideas for the finished product. Plan your kick-ass author photo to get your brain going in a different way. Whatever your genre, tumble the desired outcome with whatever sounds, words, images, textures, or even smells you can think of, and you'll dramatically pump up the magnetism of your efforts.

Little games like this help us successfully get into our feeling states and can lead to remarkable opportunities of synchronicity. Happy feeling!

You Are What You Vibrate

Have you ever noticed how wealthy people and celebrities always seem to get showered with free stuff? They receive complimentary tickets, free designer samples, meals and drinks sent over "on the house." These folks can probably easily afford all the swanky goodies coming their way, yet they're rarely asked to pay for them. When people exude the vibes of wealth, prosperity, demand, and abundance, it's almost like there's a silent pulse around them, saying, "plenty of everything, plenty of everything"—and these vibes attract more of the same. Those around them can't help but add to the coffers; it's instinctive to honor the energetic message before all else.

Alternatively, if you've ever been really strapped, you might have experienced the exact opposite. Just when you're freaking out trying to come up with rent, you run into a friend who needs that loan money back, you hear that your pending gig just fell through, and you discover a broken pipe in the kitchen that will require urgent (and pricey) repair. The energetic message of "not enough money, not enough money" exudes in perfect clarity and draws the exactly appropriate response.

If you keep seeing unwelcome patterns in your life, your energetic message clearly isn't saying what you'd like it to.

When your energetic message is nicely aligned with what you want, you'll find more delight in your daily life. (Okay, you may not notice the heavens opening every morning, but things will noticeably improve.) You'll start experiencing *instantaneous manifesting*—when a casual thought comes to fruition without any apparent effort on your part—on a regular basis. For example, you might think, "Hmm, I could go for a doughnut." And literally seconds later, you bump into a friend holding a box of doughnuts, and he or she offers you one. Just like that. And the stakes will quickly get much bigger than baked goods as you pick up steam and confidence with aligning your energy with what you want.

Alternatively, if you keep seeing unwelcome patterns in your life—delays, irritations, obstacles, disappointments—it's time to examine your vibe. Your energetic message clearly isn't saying what you'd like it to. You've got a kink, sweetheart. Maybe your positive focus isn't as positive as you think. Maybe the core desire isn't what you consciously think it is. Our results reveal the *essence* of what we're focused on, so if you're not seeing helpful occurrences and progress toward what you want, there's a problem.

Be honest with yourself about where your mind and feelings are canoodling, and when necessary, take steps to get yourself to higher energetic ground. Here's the good news: you get to start by stepping back from the intense stuff and having some more fun, for goodness sakes! If things aren't working, your little inner martyr or action addict may be acting up. Kindly remind them to just *can it*. You've got bliss to follow.

Where and When

Anytime your mind is free enough to wander, it's free for your guidance.

How do we make our energy work a habit? Where in our busy days can we find the time to put ourselves in enhanced feeling states? It's not like we're all yogis, after all. We've got stuff to *do*.

The most natural way to integrate a practice of heightened energy awareness is to use it when you need it most: when you feel the worst. "Downerville" is not the place you want to linger. *Any* shifts toward better focus areas, better emotional states, or just a better mood will help you avoid conjuring up an even more frustrating situation.

My favorite times to work on energy are when doing a minimally engaging task—say, folding laundry or taking a shower. I let my mind and heart go to town while my hands are busy, and I even incorporate the task at hand into my scenarios sometimes. I also like to directly guide my thoughts and energy right before going to sleep, as pre-sleep time is a powerful window for programming your subconscious mind (and seeding your dreams with positive expectations). Lastly, I'll work on energy whenever I'm caught in a situation that might be considered wasted time: during a traffic jam, a long line at the post office, TV commercials.

Anytime your mind is free enough to wander, it's free for your guidance.

The Jaws of Doubt

Perhaps as you've been reading the last few chapters, you've noticed yourself beginning to doubt, wondering if this kind of awareness and focus really works, or more specifically, can really work for you. Maybe the path seems too hard ("Staying conscious of my feelings *all* the time? Turning around my complaints into desires? What!?") or too easy ("Manicures and surfing? I think I'll earn my accolades the old-fashioned way—by busting my butt, thank you very much").

These doubts, even subtle ones, reveal a cynicism about the possibility of achieving our most exciting goals. After years of working tirelessly toward our dreams, and often having less than we'd like to show for it, it's easy to come to the conclusion that we may have been misguided when we set our sights so high. Perhaps our desires are the problem, we muse. Perhaps we should lower our expectations to more closely reflect a reasonable outcome.

Try *again*. Expecting less from yourself or the universe solves nothing; in fact, it will only create deeper levels of distress as you find you miss even these lower marks. You're right about one thing, though. Your expectations will *definitely* affect your outcome. And so will a number of other factors, including the way you nurture and protect your dreams along the way.

The artist's life is a special journey, full of uncommon fulfillment and unusual challenges. We frequently vacillate between extremes: fascination and aggravation, certainty and despair.

If our dreams occasionally drift out of focus, we imagine escape hatches where we abandon our art and take on a more traditional, if boring, route. We may briefly entertain the idea of surrendering to the small voice in the back of our heads suggesting we go get a "normal" job or spend our time on more "practical" pursuits. Alternatively, if our art is jamming, feeling thrillingly potent and impactful, we imagine our mark upon the world as indelible. We feel invincible, certain of our purpose and direction. In an instant, we're flowing, creating, thrilled at the possibilities unfolding before us and wondering how we could have ever imagined another life.

It takes courage to be clear about what we want, that's true. Putting desires out into the spotlight of our bright attention can be daunting, even if we're the only ones who will witness them. Deciding to direct our focus and effort toward something we really want opens us up to the risk of disappointment, the fear of

embarrassment. It also creates the *optimal conditions for our desires to come alive.*

Yes, it might feel easier sometimes to play "wait and see" and to decide that you're a passenger, instead of the driver, in your life. But it's not nearly as *fun!* Life is not nearly as exciting, as thrilling, as full of passion and amazement and accomplishment as it is when you have *actively participated* in its creation.

More Feeling-State Secrets

What conditions are you putting on your feelings? What do you think you need to have or do in order to be your best self?

Here's a tool summary to help you optimize your feeling-state endeavors.

If you're feeling *terrible*, don't try to jump straight into deep feeling-state work. That might be too great a leap for the work to do its job. Shift into a more powerful state first by doing a little self-care or something fun and light. You could sit quietly for a few minutes, change your scenery—anything really. Just get yourself into a slightly higher vibe, and *then* engage in your finale scenario or anything else you're inspired to do.

If your life seems full of situations you don't want, get them off your mind and into a better form. Try writing them all out, and then flipping them to discover exactly what you *do want.* Instead of engaging in the energy of irritation and lack, you can sigh with delight as you consider your now well-defined ideal situations. Get excited as you imagine the dramatic contrast between the way things "used to be" and the way they are "now."

If you find yourself feeling extra-aware of limitations, use the be-do-have paradigm to help you see where you might reverse the situation. What conditions are you putting on your feelings? What do you think you need to have or do in order to be your best self? Where can you embrace the feeling or being state first and let that lead to inspired actions for things to do and have?

We hunger for experience. Our souls' purpose is to learn to become *who we are* through the things and people around us, the challenges and pleasures we encounter in all we do, and, of course, the way we feel. Desire helps us discover the breadth and beauty of our spirits with more clarity and delight than anything else. As we journey forward together, I hope your desires arrive more quickly and easily than ever before. Desire's got your back. So you go get 'em, tiger.

Chapter Five: Desire

Desire arises in our lives to move us toward the people, places, things, and experiences that will fill us with happiness and purpose. What are your desires revealing about your energy?

1. Choose three of your most prominent desires and identify the core essence (feelings) you seek from them. If you're not sure, ask yourself "And then what?" until you get to the feeling level. Is there any similarity among the core essences you discover?

2. Flip three of your complaints into positive desires. No disguises allowed; make sure you're not escaping anything—only moving *toward* something you want to experience or feel.

3. Fill at least one whole piece of paper by completing the phrase "I am worthy of…" with your desires. Let 'er fly! The more desires you can come up with, the better. Just write the "I am worthy of…" part before each one. You may feel free to use other media, too; make an "I am worthy" song, cake, painting, collage, or garden—or anything else!

* **BONUS KICK-ASS CHALLENGE:** What is your dominant core energetic message? State it by starting with "I am…" Is this what you'd like it to be? Can you think of a better message to adopt and apply?

____

____

____

____

____

OPENING THE FLOW

PROJECT REC: Develop a habit of subconscious "flipping." Whenever you hear someone complain, mentally flip it into a positive want and note it to yourself, without judgment. For example, if you hear, "There are no good gigs in this town," mentally note, "Hmm, sounds like he'd love a more vibrant music scene." Done frequently enough, this exercise starts to work on us internally, so we flip our own complaints into positive desires before they even make it into verbal form.

CRAZY-EASY ROUTE: Write a glowing review for one of your current or past projects. Be as detailed or concise as you like. It can be a full-length article or a three-word quote summing it up beautifully. Direct your accolades to the aspects where you feel you really earned them. Go for the exact recognition you'd love to read about yourself.

CHAPTER SIX

Alignment

Artists care about placement and positioning.

One of the artist's gifts is the ability to know when something works—when the colors compliment or contrast each other effectively, when the notes create the perfect tonal synthesis or dissonance, when the form inhabits the space with just the right presence. The result of this careful arranging need not be *pleasing*—in fact, it often works to opposite effect to incite discussion or awareness—but it will convey *intention*. A sense of purpose and certainty exudes from fully realized works.

Artists must balance positive and negative space to find a successful tension between saturation and whiteness, sound and silence, movement and stillness. Knowing what *not* to include in a piece becomes as critical as knowing what to keep.

Working to balance *energy* this way is called alignment.

When we participate in possible paths for our desires to arrive, we relax and welcome them more fully.

Alignment requires us to stalwartly keep clear of problematic negative areas just as attentively as we craft our positive focus. For best effect, we must weed our gardens as lovingly as we plant them.

Alignment also calls for us to embrace the *havingness* of our desires. It's often easier to *want* things than to actually *have* them, so we enhance alignment by preparing for our desires. We must learn to *expect* them as certainly as we intend them to arrive. Desires inhabit space in our lives and in our identities as we integrate them into our concept of ourselves. When we are open to the actual *having*, doing the fun *receiving* gets much easier.

Lastly, alignment thrives on *possibility.* We align powerfully with our desires when we see them as truly viable. Source is capable of instantaneous manifestation, but our experience with physical matter doesn't typically support this kind of thing. So we prefer to do our part. When we participate in possible paths for our desires to arrive, we relax and welcome them more fully. When we put in time, pay our dues, and lay the groundwork with the right kind of intention, we feel much better about deserving or having earned our success.

The Artist's Teeter-Totter

One key rule of alignment is that *we can't vibrate positively and negatively at the same time.* If we are full of joy, excitement, and gratitude, our energetic space is full and fixed; there's no room for insecurity, fear, guilt, or shame. When we're hopeful and expectant, we edge out worry and inferiority. It's possible to bounce back and forth, for sure—dramatic mood swings reveal a lack of anchoring in either mindset—but it's impossible to hold strongly opposing vibrations at the same time.

Here's where we're like a teeter-totter. *Any* shift toward a positive focus can help get us off negative ground and into the realm of the flowing, feel-good side. And yep, you got it: choosing to engage with negative focus will tip you in the opposite direction.

So we are wise to protect ourselves as well as we can from anything that might tip the scales away from our happiest selves. Alignment requires our vigilance in pruning away anything that might inhibit our creative flow.

If I Had a Hammer . . .

A few years ago my husband, Mark, and I bought an old miner's house in the heart of Park City, Utah, to fix up and rent out to vacationers during the ski season. Mark is pretty handy, and most of our spare funds had gone into purchasing the house, so we were inclined to do a lot of the improvement jobs ourselves. And there were *a lot* of them to do at 24 Daly.

The house was in a terrific location, right near Main Street, but it needed a ton of work. So we got to it. While I began planning the interior finishes, materials, and furnishings, Mark started in on the heavy stuff. He opened up walls, moved doorjambs, pulled up decrepit carpeting, and tore out run-down plumbing fixtures. He was covered in dust almost every day from Halloween until Christmas.

But he was having a grand old time. Mark loves seeing how things work and using his knowledge to make them work better. He was really in his element as he ripped and sawed and hammered and fastened things. He felt confident and competent, and it showed—he seemed immensely satisfied at the end of those full days working on the Daly house, happy with his efforts and the evolving result. He was flowing like crazy as our vision for the house slowly became reality.

The part he didn't expect, however, was what would happen with the rest of his creative life. In the year or two preceding the house purchase, Mark's work as a professional stock photographer had been suffering. Media was hurting in general, and there were a lot of developing issues in the photography world with digital-rights management and copyright (basically, people were taking digital images and using them without licensing the rights). He'd

Keeping ourselves clear of the downer vibes is almost as important as pumping up the positive ones.

been inundated with doom-and-gloom reports from every industry periodical he read and meeting he attended. His personal experiences weren't much better; income was down, and it seemed that every time he opened a magazine, there was *another* photo of his that hadn't been properly licensed (which meant he had the unpleasant job of tracking down the infringing party for the appropriate fees). He was carrying a low-grade anxiety most days, going something like, "What am I going to do for work if stock photography continues to suffer? How can I constantly watch thousands of publications for infringements? This is so unfair. I've worked so hard for this and now everything is falling apart!"

His focus was filled with helplessness. He felt overwhelmed, overpowered, and uncertain of his next steps. But when he began working on the Daly house, he began feeling sure of himself again. He knew what needed to be done, and he knew how to do it. He felt powerful and effective again. He got excited about what was happening. His valve had been opened.

And guess what happened?

The great energy Mark was summoning through his home-improvement work started spilling over into his work life, too. He started noticing that photography sales were coming in better and more often than they had in the past, even though he was spending less time than ever in the office. And they were easy sales—no haggling, no huge file editing; just straightforward requests from great clients with good budgets.

While preparing for taxes at the end of the year, Mark was shocked to discover that the three months he'd been working on the Daly house had been his highest earning quarter in years (and probably the least time intensive for his photo work).

The vibes he put out while in that terrifically competent zone certainly attracted great clients and uses, but I also suspect that the *lack* of negative energy contributed significantly to the remarkable jump in income. Keeping ourselves clear of the downer vibes is almost as important as pumping up the positive ones.

Think of it this way: if we're putting hot water into a tub but also adding cool water, we'll never get a gorgeous, steaming bath;

it will always remain tepid. But if we allow the cold water to drain away, the tub is clear and ready for the all the warm, swirling wonderfulness we might want.

Living Clear

We sometimes attach a moral component to deserving success. It's probably a holdover from the religious dogma or bootstrap mentality of our forefathers that tells us, "Work hard, and be good, and you'll earn your rewards." So it becomes totally irritating when we see all kinds of rewards going to people who apparently haven't worked very hard or been very good.

Here's what happened: they didn't *need* to labor day and night or to uphold rock-solid ethics, because they were *aligned* with what they wanted. They were clear on it; they maintained a fab focus, prepared for its arrival, and expected it to come. It may not have even occurred to them to get tied up in the "Am I worthy?" ruminations or the "How will I deal with that kind of success?" questions that can trip up the more sensitive among us.

Morals do matter, but probably not in the way that you think. *Moral conflict* interferes with alignment; it's guilt or worry or shame that constricts our connection to Source more than our specific actions. If you're completely sure that you acted in the proper spirit, you're fine. You still have alignment. Issues of living "clear" start to show when guilt or worry or shame start distracting us or becoming negative vibes that keep us from what we want.

Here's an example. You write a great song and later discover that there's a part of the melody that's similar to one in a famous song. It happened inadvertently, and once you discover it, you adjust the melody a little to make it more clearly your own.

Perhaps later you find yourself worrying about it, unsure if you changed it enough. You start worrying that you have no original ideas. You feel guilty. *Your negative focus takes you out of alignment, and both you and the song are affected by the negative vibration.* This kind of situation leads to reduced opportunities for you and the

song itself. Maybe you don't submit it to a song contest because you worry that it's still too close to the other melody and you'll be called out for plagiarism. Or you resist playing it in public because you feel funny about it. It can end up burying the song for you.

On the other hand, perhaps you decide the revision worked. You feel good about it; you like the song and if anything, the changes made it stronger. You remind yourself that we hear other people's songs subconsciously all the time, and it's not unthinkable that a snippet here or there might occasionally end up in a new piece until we notice it. It even happened to George Harrison once, so why not you? You feel great and productive, and *remain in perfect alignment*. You add the song to your repertoire and send it off to whatever opportunities you can find. The song wins a competition, and you get to perform it for thousands of people.

In both cases, it was the *feelings*, and how they were honored or not, that affected the course of action and eventual alignment. Our actions attract the exact results that align with our vibrations.

Living clean and clear—morally and fairly, with ethical clarity in our personal and business lives—allows us to keep clear of the little energy drains that affect our vibrations (and the vibrations of our work). So if you're not sure if you *really* want to return that doubled royalty payment, download that pirated graphic-design software, or forward your friend's new record to that bigshot music supervisor as you offered, you might want to consider it more seriously—for the sake of your vibrations.

Havingness and Gremlins

Another element of alignment is preparing for the actuality of our desires in our lives. In forming our desires, we examine the details. Do I actually want this, or do I just like the idea of it? Can I really live with the schedule that a job like that would entail? What would happen if I actually got to tour the world and play sold-out arenas every night?

Aligning with *havingness* requires a delicate touch. Getting into strong feeling states requires that we imagine our desire as fully as possible; we must expand and embrace our senses to make the desire as real as we can. We're creative, broad thinkers: it's understandable if negative elements occasionally enter the picture in our minds. We can call these little irritants *gremlins.*

Gremlins love to creep in and niggle at us just as we're getting excited about a new desire. "I want to earn tons of money with my next film," we think, and the gremlin says, "Yeah, but then your brothers are going to soak you for cash all the time." Or we decide, "I want to take a trip around the world!" And our gremlin chimes in, "Hope you like dysentery!"

The annoying part about gremlins is that they're usually working from a grain of truth or touching on a hot-button part of our identity. They'll cut us off before we even embrace a desire if there's some inner conflict to stir up. "I couldn't possibly want that camera," we say, before we've even really considered it. "It's far too expensive!" Or maybe we have different reasons, such as, "I'm not technically minded and won't ever learn to use it" or "I'm just a beginner and will look stupid with such an advanced model."

To create more havingness for your desires, it's necessary to disarm the gremlins by getting right in their faces with our power tools. Rrrrrrrr! Use your focus, finale thinking, and shifting to imagine the best possible results instead of the worst ones. Here lies the only exception to our rule of resisting any negative focus: deal with gremlins head on. When neglected, they have a tendency to grow disturbingly large.

Preparing for your desire to come into your life in its full, actual glory will help you welcome it with unfettered excitement. You're allowed to both have what you want and *love it*, too.

You're allowed to both have what you want and *love it*, too.

Plant Your Seeds

A sense of *possibility* keeps our energies exceptionally high and aligned.

When we put ourselves out there, as the saying goes, all those wonderful desires of ours floating around out there can find us. We feel like we see a clearer relationship between action and reward.

We expand possibility in our lives by planting the seeds of our desires.

We like to feel involved in the specific paths our desires take to us, even if it's not really necessary from a universal point of view. It makes us feel like we're not just choosing the music, but also dancing.

We expand possibility in our lives by planting the seeds of our desires. When we extend ourselves and embrace opportunities, there are increasingly more ways we can realistically imagine the things we want coming into our lives. Our participation in the process activates a sense of expectation that pumps up our energy with purpose and vitality.

So start planting. Anytime you're touched by inspiration, honor it. Mention your desire for a new studio to your friends. Reserve a booth at the upcoming art fair, even if your pieces aren't all ready yet. Enter contests or competitions. Mail out beautiful packets introducing your work to industry professionals. Send brief, charming emails to your professional contacts from time to time. Sign up for portfolio reviews. Write a letter of introduction and appreciation to one of your artistic idols.

Stretch. Ask your idol to mentor you. Take a class for which you're barely qualified. Make a call that makes your heart race. Audition for the ridiculously intimidating show. Your risk determines your rewards: the higher the stakes, the more spectacular the possibilities.

The more seeds you plant, the better. You never know which ones are going to flower, and which might just need to germinate for a while until they can pop up some other sunny spring day. Besides, it's harder to slow things down with worry or fear if there are too many possibilities to remember individually. You want to stay light and open for anything, not caught up in some rigid attachment to a particular way a desire might arrive in your life.

You're shooting for a state of constant, but loose expectation. Today could be the day that *anything* happens! You might hear from the director of that workshop in Italy, or the editor of that national magazine, or the judging committee to let you know you've been named a finalist. If you regularly plant your seeds (and continue to nurture any cute little seedlings that begin to grow) any day can truly be that day.

Expand It: Be the Change You Want to See

Expansion enhances alignment.

We beckon in more of what we want to experience when we recognize that we already have it, if even just in a small way. (Stay with me here. I hear you saying, "But I *don't* have it! That's the problem!" I could be wrong, but I think you actually *do* have some, or you wouldn't want more.) Look for the little nuggets you already have. These are happy little trial-size portions from the universe letting you know that if you are conscious with a little, you can expand it into a *lot*. Those familiar with Bible stories might think of this kind of expansion as an artistic form of the loaves and the fishes. When we share with others, we display faith in the concept of *enough*. We let go. We stop hoarding and constricting, and allow the wonderful current of abundance to pick us up and move us forward. And we begin to witness a great new sense of bounty.

When we share with others, we display faith in the concept of *enough*.

So be proactive about it. Decide what you want more of, and figure out how you can expand on the parts you already have to create more of its energy in your life. *Be the change you want to experience in your life and the world.* Be generous. Work from the biggest part of your spirit, the part above any pettiness or ego, and you'll immediately start to feel a difference in your own resources.

If you want to find more helpful contacts in your field, make a concerted effort to share some helpful contacts with an emerging artist who crosses your path. Help your peers: add a page to your website with links to the sites of peers you respect. Give a leg up by offering your time and expertise to organizations that nurture promising artists in your field.

If you'd like more funding for your work, share the resources you have with someone else who might need them *even more than*

you do. Donate some of your extra art supplies to a homeless shelter. Toss a heftier handful of change into a busker's guitar case. Offer to perform a free show or teach a class for a school with a limited (or nonexistent) arts program.

Do you want more support? Affection? Time? Give more of these to the people around you. Write a note with the top ten things you love most about your honey, best friend, or family member, and mail (or email) it to them. Give a hug to someone who you normally wouldn't. Make a meal for a friend who's overwhelmed. Call your neighbor and offer to take the kids to the park for an hour.

Want to feel you matter in the world? That you're making an impact? Smile with real sincerity at the checkout clerk. Look strangers in the eye. Let someone go ahead of you in line if they seem rushed. Be playful with nearby kids. Take note of how another person's small gesture has affected you recently, and let them know how much you appreciate it.

You'll figure it out. Your creativity will guide you.

I'll warn you: the early phases of this one can be hard. When we're deep in lack mode, one of our favorite pastimes tends to be a game of "Whose fault is this?" (We rarely consider our own involvement while in those really dark moments). You'll probably find yourself guided to reach out to exactly the people with whom you're most frustrated. "But why should I support my wife when she doesn't support me?" you might think. Or "How can I offer my business contacts to that jerk? He never offers me any of his!" It might help to remember this is about *your* energy, not theirs. Maintaining the energetic identity of a generous, competent, supported, abundant, acclaimed artist allows you to share without fear.

Still not convinced? Consider the alternative! Would you rather embrace the identity of the whiney, worried, strapped, tight, ignored, and fearful artist who clutches to every crumb of an opportunity as if it's his last? Would you rather live from the precipice of failure? *Hell, no!* Who wants that?

Fun, Light, Frisky, and Free!

Finally, we align brilliantly when we have *fun*.

One of the most effective sentences I've found for increasing energy around something I want is the simple statement "*That* might be fun." This easy-going, happy-go-lucky little announcement has yielded me exotic trips, hip technological gadgets, swanky fashion items, delightful romances, weekend workshops—even fun guest spots on TV shows. As someone who's been as steeped as the next person in the idea that we need to work hard to get what we want, it was almost unnerving to find things dropping into my lap with such ease and little effort.

What if we let ourselves believe it's *always* light, fun, frisky, and free?

So why would a light little phrase like this work so well?

It took me ages to realize why, but now it seems clear why it works so quickly and effectively. When I notice something and lightly say to myself, "That might be fun!" I'm aligning in three ways. I'm:

1. Focusing my attention on something positive, desired, and pleasurable;
2. Allowing myself to feel some loose, fun enthusiasm as I imagine enjoying it;
3. Staying clear of negative vibes. I'm not particularly attached to anything about this situation (exactly how or when it's going to happen, for instance), and since it's just a light request, I don't worry about it or create any resistant concerns.

And you know what happens? My fun desire arrives. It arrives in silly ways, incredible ways, and faster than I could imagine if I dictated its path myself.

What if we let ourselves believe it's *always* light, fun, frisky, and free? Let's keep it loose and fun as we go about the process of using our energy to attract what we want (especially since that's what, umm, *works*). The moment we lay the heavy tone of "very

important, very serious creation at work here" (imagine a deep voice), we tighten up the all-important valve of wonderful loving warm energy. Our expanded self is fantastically good humored and joyful; this energy fills us and informs our experience more and more deeply as when we enjoy a relaxed, happy vibration.

In my creative retreats, the light, fun, frisky, and free energy can really get zipping around. A women's weekend that we held last year began with a bang; those women were *really happy* to be there. The group was small and focused, and most of the women had busy families that they'd left at home in order to concentrate on bringing some personal creative dreams to life. There was instant bonding and lively layers of animated conversation. Support, ideas, and resources flowed freely and generously. It was as if the floodgates were opening up and the whole studio began to light up with a happy energy.

We began to work at art stations around the space, allowing everyone to play with paint, make jewelry, or do other activities as they worked independently or chatted with one another. Much of the conversation centered on projects the women were working on or ideas they hoped to develop over the weekend, but naturally other topics came into play as well. We talked about the great books we were reading, inspiring info we'd come across on TV shows or the Web, delicious meals we had recently enjoyed, and the supportive help of those who had made the weekend possible for each of us. There was much laughter and nodding as the sharing and creative projects continued.

As the vibration got higher and higher in the room, fascinating examples of instant manifestation began to take place. It started small: one woman mentioned that she loved the "Miracle Muffins" that they made at a local health-food store, but hadn't had time to stop and pick any up. Just then another woman got a big smile on her face and pulled out a bag of those exact muffins to share. Someone pulled out a fascinating-looking book about elements of healing and creativity. Carrie mentioned that she'd love to read something like that, and it occurred to me that I should take a quick look in my car. (I had recently been to a library book sale and had a box of all kinds of titles that had looked interesting sitting in the back of my wagon.) I went to the car, opened the box, pulled the exact book out that Carrie had been eyeing, and gave it to her to enjoy for as long as she wanted it.

Then we started talking about the Kindle, a cool, lightweight digital "e-reader" that had recently been featured on a popular talk show. I said (the now-magic words), "Wow, yeah! That might be fun!" We continued to chat about how useful and convenient it might be, and how it would bring a cool, new pleasurable element to the simple act of reading books. *And less than an hour later*, my sister called me to tell me that she wanted to get me this Kindle reader for a birthday present, and would this be something that I might enjoy?! I couldn't believe it.

When I reviewed the afternoon in my mind, however, I realized something astonishing: *I couldn't recall a single negative comment.* One by one, our requests were met in delightful, easy ways, as we managed to stay out of the territory of lower-vibe thoughts or comments. The energy was so lovely and high in the room that I think it just edged out typical negative responses, leaving the flow fast and free and ready to deliver whatever it might be that just "might be fun."

Chapter Six: Alignment

Aligning with our desires helps us keep the paths clear. This is the territory of getting out of our own way.

1. Where are you tethered down? When our desires have strings (or weights!) attached, it's much more difficult to bring them to life. Let's get snipping those sandbags! Create a before-and-after representation of your energetic tethers and their symbolic release. Choose a visual or tactile approach, or

involve elements of ritual or gesture. Use balloons, bubbles, scarves, leaves, smoke, baby powder, or anything else that sounds fun.

2. Where can you find evidence that you already have one of your desires (at some level)? Can you expand it by demonstrating it to someone else or sharing your resources?

3. Is there one area of your life where your gremlins tend to attack most frequently? If you discovered tomorrow that your limiting belief wasn't true—that for instance, you *do* deserve a management position—how would that change your desires?

* **BONUS KICK-ASS CHALLENGE:** Are you struggling with any gray areas as far as living clean? If you've been tangled in any moral dilemmas, decide today to either take the high road or find a way to get okay with your choice.

Opening the Flow

Project Rec: Plant some seeds, both literally and figuratively. Plant twenty seeds or flowers representing the nurturing and patience you are offering your creative spirit. Now make a list of twenty things you could do to enhance your sense of possibility. Be specific—list people you might contact, events or competitions you might register or apply for, anything that could bring an exciting result can go on the list. Then for the next week, each day choose at least one item on your list and do it. Don't allow yourself to get caught up in small obstacles. (For instance, if you don't have your favorite author's address, send it to the publisher.) If you're aspiring to be an energy rock star, you can choose to do all the items on your list. Care for your seedlings and see their daily growth as a metaphor for your other rich possibilities taking hold.

Crazy-Easy Route: Cultivate a loose, easy detachment from desire. The next time you see something that looks like it would be fun to do or have, consciously say to yourself—out loud, if possible—"That would be fun!" Repeat it: "Yeah! That looks like fun!" Then forget it and move on with your happy day.

CHAPTER SEVEN

ALLOWING

As artists, we're *givers.*

Our mission is to express, contribute, create. We integrate, interpret, render. Our sense of purpose and value can often seem directly related to output. We keep a running tally on ourselves: How am I producing? Is this any good? Do I have anything new or really valuable to say? Is this more evolved than my last work? Will anyone care?

We stand on stages or open our mouths or lay ourselves on the page or canvas, saying: "Here I am. Here's what I've got. I offer it to you. You can share it." We are incredibly brave—often in the face of profound fear. But we believe there is something important to say, and for whatever reason, *we* are the ones to say it. And so we do.

When our creations seem ready—hard as it is to tell sometimes—we send them off to find their place in the world. We hold them close in our last moments together, as if they

We are givers. And this is exactly why so very many of us have trouble with *allowing*.

are our little children heading for the big yellow bus, and whisper, "Be good! Have fun!" We hope they'll make us proud, though we continue to love them if they don't.

In order to create, we must become comfortable with the birthing of ideas into form. We steward tiny sparks into fire, nurture seeds into little plants and sometimes mighty trees. We face the vast whiteness of the yet-to-be-created and emerge whole, stronger, sometimes victorious in our thrilling results. And even when the whiteness seems to prevail, leaving us uncertain of our abilities or potency, we return to try again. We *believe* in what we have to offer. We have to.

We are givers. And this is exactly why so very many of us have trouble with *allowing*.

The art of allowing is the ability of opening ourselves to receive.

Most of us imagine that we'd be great at receiving, if only given the chance to experience it. We suppose that the abundance and acclaim and incredible opportunities that we crave are kept out of our reach because of personal limitations: "I'm not skilled enough, innovative enough, young enough, good-looking enough, old enough." We might wonder if we're not good enough at working with our energy even, or keeping a positive enough attitude, or visualizing with enough clarity and detail.

But haven't you ever noticed people who seem to find fantastic success *without* the perfect resume that many of us assume is necessary to "make it?" How does Tom Petty—an unusual-looking guy with a nontraditional voice—sell tens of millions of albums and chart eighteen top-ten hits? How does Jean-Michel Basquiat, a kid from Brooklyn with no formal art training, rise to the top of the New York art scene and find himself, at twenty-two, at the center of the new Neo-Expressionist movement? How does Helen Hoover Santymeyer write her first novel, *And the Ladies of the Club,* at ninety years old and delightedly watch it top the bestseller lists?

Examples like this help underscore that it's not the *conditions* of our lives that create happiness and opportunities. It's our energy. If we waited patiently for every element in our subjective experience to line up perfectly before we take our creative leaps, we'd all be waiting around forever! Nothing would *ever* get written or built or painted or sung or programmed or performed or invented, and our world would feel awfully *beige.*

GREAT BALLS OF FIRE

When I was starting out as a songwriter, I attended SongSchool, a great camp in Lyons, Colorado, for emerging writers and artists. The faculty was amazing, and they did a terrific job of covering the basics of songwriting and playing, along with the more subtle, but still quite important, elements of energy.

The *best* experiences are created when the performer and audience *both* send and receive.

During one session, the instructor asked us to stand up, choose a partner, and pretend to throw a ball back and forth between us. We were to imagine that the ball was a precious, heavy orb.

I started tossing it back and forth with my partner. There were some chuckles as we all started really engaging with the exercise, sometimes running after our imaginary balls as they rolled away or were lobbed too far overhead.

After a few minutes, the instructor asked us to stop and give our feedback on how it felt to toss the ball and to catch it. The overwhelming reaction was that it was very straightforward to throw the ball, but much harder to catch it. We all felt fairly comfortable with the impression of the ball's weight and momentum as we originated the toss, but a little silly and uncertain of ourselves as we went through the motions of receiving it.

The brilliant instructor then connected the exercise to the relationship between performer and audience. She told us:

> As performers, we get really good at sending *out* our energy. We send it, send it, send it, and that's great. Audience members come to absorb—that's part of their role, and they know it. But the *best* experiences are created when there's a complete circuit—a loop of energy—when the performer and audience *both* send and receive.

> It might start before you, as the performer, even come onstage. Maybe it begins when you hear and feel the anticipation of the crowd and allow that to fill you with excitement. Then when you step onstage and begin to play, you allow your heightened excitement to flow through the music out into the crowd. As the audience begins to respond to your words and music, *you allow them to send the energy right back into you.* You receive it and flow it back out again. And around it goes. You feel heard and appreciated. But the *audience also* feels heard and appreciated.
>
> This circuit is what makes for life-changing shows. This is what leaves you wired and high after playing or attending a concert like this. The shared experience is the richest one.

This exercise and wisdom has affected me so much over the years as I've performed and attended concerts (that have gone both thrillingly well and train-wreck awful, for the record). But as I consider it in relation to the art of allowing, I realize how much we, as givers, can always use extra practice at receiving. We need to be just as sure of ourselves when we catch as when we throw. As we go about our days, every day, brilliant orbs of energy are metaphorically showering down all around us in the form of fantastic opportunities, glimmers of intuition, the exact perfect contacts we're seeking, and we merely need to learn to catch them.

The Artist's Toy Store

Here's another way to look at how the energy of allowing works.

Say you've been surfing around the Web and found a great site called "The Artist's Toy Store" (*www.theartiststoystore.com)*. There you find the *perfect* thing—exactly what you need for a current project. It's feels *possible* for you (it's affordable and would fit in your studio), you *like it* (it looks like fun to use), you're *excited* about it (you're already thinking about how useful and cool it will be), and so you decide, "Yes! I want it!"

You select the item and put it in your virtual shopping cart. You go to the checkout page and fill out the information—where it should be shipped, how you would like to pay, how soon you need it, and so on. When you're done, you click "buy," and it's on its way, right? Right.

Unless you mess with the order. Maybe you can't decide, so you wait to press "buy," and your page expires or your connection is lost. Or you do click "buy," but then decide you should've checked to see if it came in different colors, so you press the "back" button before the transaction has gone through. Or you don't know why it's taking so long to get to a confirmation email, so you click "buy" several more times without waiting for the results. Or maybe you contact customer service before the order has even gone through to see what's happening and why it's not showing up in your email yet. Or perhaps you even got a confirmation email, but you keep checking in with customer service on a daily basis because your package still hasn't arrived (even though it's not due for another day). You see where we're going with this, yes?

When doubt, indecision, or impatience creep into our energy work, things get complicated.

These are the pitfalls we avoid when we skillfully use *allowing* to make room for our desires to show up in our lives. Getting what we want can be as straightforward as ordering it. We initiate the process by taking three steps: deciding our want is possible/pleasurable/positive for us, indicating that we want it, and outlining specifics of delivery (or remembering that our info is all "on file" with the universe). Then we simply trust that it's on its way, and we wait excitedly for it to arrive. It's when doubt, indecision, or impatience creep into our energy work that things get more complicated than they need to be. Trust is what keeps us clear of the elements that lock up our process and keeps the valve to all that's possible wide open.

With Open Arms . . .

So how can we train ourselves to trust, to catch the exciting opportunities and goodies we've ordered up from the universe? How can

we become better at allowing, become so natural at it so that it's our default state, not something we're always working to remember?

There are four keys to allowing that will help it become a daily habit and get your life and art sparking. You can remember these four elements with the fab mnemonic device HEAT, which stands for:

1. Higher vibes
2. Expectation
3. Acting on inspiration
4. Thanks!

Step 1: Higher Vibes

Keep your vibes high and happy. When you notice them weighing down or swirling around negative town (a good hint is that you're using the words *no, not, don't, won't, can't,* or *never* a lot), use the *don't wants* to guide you straight into the higher-vibed arms of your *do wants.* Use your favorite shifting techniques—self-care, meditation, exercise, getting into the feeling states of your want, or anything else you find helpful to lift you up, up, up into a zone that feels *good.*

If you're having some trouble and are *really* caught up in a negative mindset, you may try to be a hero and jump from hopeless and desperate to joyful and thrilled. Resist this urge if you can. When we attempt to force our feelings into submission, the shift doesn't feel authentic, which can make us feel even worse. Our feelings tend to settle in one zone of a continuum and to move in waves more than leaps. (This works in both directions: When we're feeling great, very little seems to bother us. When we're feeling really crummy, even great news won't seem to penetrate.)

So if you're not happy with how you're feeling, ask yourself if you're ready to let go of feeling the way you do. If you *aren't,* in fact, ready, take some time to figure out what might be serving you from your current downer way of thinking by asking yourself what

you're getting out of it. Is it sympathy? Attention? Camaraderie? Then resolve whether the benefits are truly helping you right now or if you'd *really* rather have your want. If you *are* ready to move on, you don't have to cross the Grand Canyon of emotions—just find a place that feels *better* than the place where you are.[7]

You don't have to cross the Grand Canyon of emotions—just find a place that feels *better* than the place where you are.

For instance, if you currently feel frustrated, perhaps you'll find that with some shifting, you can get to *irritated.* (Irritated isn't great, but it's better than frustrated.) From there, you might find yourself able to shift up into merely *annoyed.* Then *empathetic.* Then perhaps *compassionate.* Then *excited.* And *trusting.* And so on. You just keep on keeping on until you find yourself in a much, much higher vibration than what you were feeling just a brief time ago.

Well, At Least…

One method for ascending the scale to better emotional states is to use the "Well, At Least" method of shifting. It's kind of a back-door way into gratitude and can be especially helpful when you really don't feel like being thankful.

Here's an example of how it might unfold. Say you've been working for six months on a collection of really great new greeting cards to present to a card company where you have a contact. Everything's all set up, your prototypes are finally ready, but when you call to confirm the meeting, you discover that your contact has left the company! There will be no meeting, no presentation, and since you can't seem to reach your contact at all at the moment, you don't know how you're going to move forward at all! All the work you did in preparation feels like a waste. All the *talking* you did about it to friends and family makes you feel like a fool. You are frustrated. You're angry, even! This is not the way you imagined (and even visualized, dang it!) this happening.

So you have a choice. You can wallow for a bit. (As I've mentioned before, I'm not proud of my wallowing tendencies, but I

7. In the Esther and Jerry Hicks/Abraham book *Ask and It Is Given* (Carlsbad, CA, Hay House, 2005), there's a substantial discussion of the emotional scale and strategies for ascending it.

certainly acknowledge that they exist.) You can decide to get really deep down in the muck of it—calling your friends to discuss the depths of disappointment you feel and how lame this guy was for not letting you know his situation was changing and what will you do with these stupid cards now, and so on.

Or right away (or as soon as you're ready), you can decide to start shifting up the emotional scale.

Maybe your first thought could be something like, "**Well, at least** I didn't get all dressed up tomorrow and go all the way down there to hear the bad news. It was good that I called to confirm, I guess." Something like this might bring you out of the "I'm an idiot" mindset and into the "Well, I did do *some* things right" state of mind, leaving you less *frustrated* and closer to *irritated*.

Perhaps from there you might starting thinking, "**Well, at least** I *finished* the cards. That was a project I was trying to get done for a long time, and the deadline helped me stay focused, even if no one will get to see them for awhile." So here you might make the step from *irritated* to merely *annoyed*.

Then maybe you'll think about your friend for a moment. "I wonder what's happening with him? I wonder why he chose to leave, or worse, if he was fired. **Well, at least** I'm self-employed and don't have to worry about being fired. That would be rough." And you'd move from *annoyed* to *empathetic*.

And then perhaps you might nurture your empathy for your contact. "I hope he's all right. Gosh, he had so many projects going, and he was really helpful in developing my card line. He probably feels terrible that things worked out this way. **Well, at least** maybe I could track him down through his nice assistant, and let him know I heard about the change and will figure out some other options—not to worry about me." And you'd be shifting into *compassionate*.

It might be at this stage, at a much higher vibration than your earlier frustration, that you start getting some pings of ideas for inspired action. Maybe you start thinking, "Wow, you know, Jeannie's been asking me to bring some samples of my cards into her shop. Maybe I could do that since they're all ready. And oh, she's part of that independent booksellers network. I wonder how many of them might be interested in these new cards. They *are* pretty distinctive, and I'd make more money if I distributed them myself. Maybe I'll call her right now."

When one of your inspired actions leads to an even better situation than you initially imagined, you just might find yourself in a state of *trust*. Suddenly, it's clearer that the universe has your best interests at heart. Suddenly, the timing of your contact's departure feels more like a blessing than a tragedy. Suddenly, the *conditions* of the cancelled meeting aren't negative anymore, because your *energy* isn't negative anymore.

Step 2: Cultivate Expectation and Belief

Remember our good pal possibility? Expectation is her best friend.

Find ways to stoke your sense of expectation. When we clearly state our desires, we pave the way for their arrival; it's only by changing our minds about what we want or getting in the way (by stirring up negative or conflicting energy around them) that our desires get detoured or delayed. To keep the paths clear and our wants happily speeding their way into our lives, it's important to *believe that they're coming* and to *create room for them* in our lives, both literally and figuratively.

One way of creating movement and stimulation in our lives is to declutter and beautify our environment.

Feng shui practitioners frequently discuss the importance of the flow of energy through our spaces. When clutter gathers in certain areas of our homes or surroundings, they explain, the *qi*, or life force, becomes stagnant and clogged in corresponding specific areas of our lives. So one way of creating movement and stimulation in a facet of our lives is to declutter and beautify the parallel section of our environment. Feng shui also suggests that we can pump up energy through the conscious use of color, textures, and shapes. (Ooh baby! Crafty, creative types like us can go nuts as we intentionally arrange and decorate our spaces for maximum energy.)

Learning about this aspect of feng shui has brought a wonderful new element to my (previously uninspired) housekeeping.

- When I want to pump up some prosperity, I might put some extra love into the kitchen (which happens to be the abundance sector of our home). Keeping it clear and sparkling is one way to get the ball rolling on some monetary mojo.
- If I'm craving more awareness or acknowledgment of my work, I might spruce up the dining room (our fame and recognition sector). I'll shine up the table, hang pretty things in the windows, and get a dramatic, colorful spiky plant for the centerpiece.
- If I'd like some extra help with my business contacts, I'll take a closer look at what's been accumulating in the media room/library (our helpful people sector) and spend some time making sure it feels free of any clutter, cobwebs, or dust. I might write down the names of people whose help I'd like and fold them into pretty origami birds for the end table. (And hope that Daisy manages to leave them in place for at least a day.)

Use intention with your spaces—set them up for the life you want.

Pick a part of your home that's clogged with clutter, and as you clear it out, decide what result you'd like to see from your efforts. For instance, as you clean your car, you might say, "I'm going places!" As you clean your attic, you might decide, "There's no cap on what I might accomplish." (Your intentions needn't be as cheesy as my examples, by the way.)

Feng shui experts also suggest that you use intention with your spaces—set them up for the life you want, not just the life you are currently living.

Say you'd like to start working with a great writing partner. You might start preparing for the arrival your ideal partner in both practical and symbolic ways. Check out a feng shui *bagua* (chart) and find the area of your space that corresponds to the idea of partnerships for you.[8] Clean it up, pitch the junk, move stuff around, deal with anything that's been there for ages. Start highlighting the concept of pairs. Put two chairs or a double desk in your office. Arrange a duo of candles on the table. Choose artwork and interior design elements in balanced pairs. Visualize how it will look as you and your partner work happily. Then start imagining the great work you'll accomplish and how easy and flowing it will feel. Finally, take a moment to examine your current relationships, too. If you're allowing an old, unproductive partnership to limp along when its time has clearly passed, you're not doing anyone any favors. Let it go, clear it out, make room for new energy, and believe in better possibilities for *all* parties involved.

Manifesting pioneer Florence Scovel Schinn concurs that demonstrating faith through concrete actions hastens the arrival of your desire. If you desire a big check in the mail, for instance, she advocates buying a beautiful letter opener with which to greet the exciting envelope. If you're hoping for a new car, make room in your garage for the car to fit beautifully.

We *expect* our desires to have a specific impact upon our lives—it's part of their appeal. As we prepare for their arrival in concrete ways, we also remove little energetic obstacles. As long as we feel good about it, welcoming our wants in tangible ways is a terrific way to allow them to come more quickly and easily.

So often it seems our desires take their sweet time showing up, which starts us distractedly worrying and wondering what's going on. It can be hard to tell whether the universe is merely fine-tuning the timing or if there are some major glitches in our energetic welcome mat. Whatever the case it might be, as we wait, it can help to feel we're at least in preparation mode for arrival.

This isn't muscling or panic—this is faith at work.

8. For the most fun and accessible examples I've come across about applying feng shui techniques to your life, check out Karen Rauch Carter's terrific book *Move Your Stuff, Change Your Life: How to Use Feng Shui to Get Love, Money, Respect and Happiness* (New York: Fireside, 2000).

This is trust. It's "I know it's coming. I know it's being crafted especially for me in perfect time and form. And so I'm showing my appreciation in advance by letting it be known that I'm ready and excited."

Step 3: Acting on Inspiration

When we start raising our energy and vibration, amazing things begin happening. Helpful coincidences start to seem commonplace. Synergies happen all over the place. Little urges or nudges seem to come to mind more clearly, and we find ourselves in the right place at the right time ridiculously often. Things start to feel *easier*. We are relaxed, trusting. We notice that there just seems to be plenty of everything to go around.

Acting on inspiration allows our physical selves to do the work of our higher Source.

Acting on inspiration allows our physical selves to do the work of our higher Source. When we're tapped into Big Creative, we're an effective channel for not only the ideas of our expanded creator self, but also the opportunity to serve others and ourselves. When our energy is high and clear, we feel more able to step up to help and be more generous with our resources and gifts.

In low energy and vibration, life feels slow and heavy—like we're moving through gelatin instead of air. Every transaction seems fraught with delays and complications. We feel that the universe is conspiring *against* us. It's one thing after another. We are suspicious of other people's motives. We are tight, constricted in both mind and body. We hoard.

But mostly, we get tired. It seems like *way* too much effort to make changes or adjustments in our own lives, let alone to reach out to help others. We barely feel like instruments of our own thoughts and needs, let alone the extension of a greater power.

So we begin to muscle it. Have you ever heard the gory stories about how chickens can still run around after their heads have been cut off? It's kind of like that. When we lose our connection to Source, we experience only a frantic, panicky kind of energy. We lose sense of where we are or where we're headed, so we just flail around. We knock stuff over, stir things up, and try to get somewhere—anywhere—other than where we are. Our nervous system takes over and our muscles jump in, but our head is nowhere to be found.

These are uninspired actions. This is us when we resort to lowering all our prices in a desperate attempt to get someone (anyone) to finally buy something. Or drunken dialing an old, unfulfilling partner and begging to get back together. Or angrily shooting off a livid email to that critic or gallery owner who didn't immediately see the value in our work. Or going online to see about those gigs that sound like a nightmare, but would pay the bills. You get the picture.

When we act from a place of distress and panic, the valve that connects us to Source is constricted. We're largely on our own, stripped of the fantastically big-picture assistance that is possible with our potent, Big Creative partner. As we chug along on our own efforts alone, we can see only the small bit of road ahead of us—not the pile-up in the distance, the hail storm that'll cross our path tomorrow, or the major highway reconstruction coming up next week. We feel blindsided by the crap that keeps hitting our windshield, and we are. We're missing the guidance and help that's always available to us by choosing a higher vibration and opening our valve to Source.

How can we make sure we're acting on inspiration, rather than out of desperation? For one thing, ask yourself about the state you were in when the idea struck you for this action. Were you feeling good—excited, content, grateful, relaxed, joyful? Or were you feeling worried, anxious, frustrated, helpless, or another negative state? Were you relatively calm with a quiet mind, or ruminating through lists in your head for ways to solve this problem intellectually? Does the idea excite you in its long-term possibilities, or does it seem like a stopgap measure? Does it energize you in a warm-fuzzy way or a too-much-coffee way? If you could bounce the idea off a person or two that you trust, do you imagine their responses would be positive or negative?

We create the ideal state for inspired action when there is positive energy flowing; a calm, clear mind to "hear" the guidance; and a state of true ease with the present. When we trust that things will be okay—no matter what conditions indicate—we are able

to more clearly see the paths for *making* them okay. And in this state, we're able to take the time and effort to act on inspiration, quickly and directly. There's no need to mess around; real guidance usually comes with clarity, specificity, and a surge of motivation. It feels like: "Ah! *I know*. This is what I'll do. Here's how I'll do it. Right now."

Real guidance usually comes with clarity, specificity, and a surge of motivation.

Step 4: Thanks!

The last, and possibly easiest and most lovely, step in allowing is gratitude.

Have you ever watched the way little kids respond to receiving a toy they really want? The excitement begins to build before they've even opened the present. "I think it might be _______!" they say, with bated breath, to anyone listening. As they peel back the gift wrap and see their desired toy, the excitement floods their faces and bodies with thrilled energy as they imagine all the fun they'll have. They can't contain themselves, and they hop up to run around or jump up and down or dance, clutching the toy as they say over and over how much they wanted it and how glad they are to finally have it. This is usually where a parent chimes in the obligatory, "And *what do you say*?" To which the kid suddenly halts—if the parent's lucky—to say a brief, dutiful, "thank youuu" to the giver before racing off to play with the new toy that they obviously love.

We could learn a lot from kids.

They are not shy about declaring what they want. They're not particularly concerned with who will get it for them or how it'll be wrapped. They will remind those in charge of what is it they want, often (sometimes several times a day). They can remain excited about the object of their desire for a *very* long time. They sense its imminent arrival and will declare *that too* to those around them. And when they get what they want, they accept it! They love it! They open up that sucker and start playing with it! They experience pure joy—and immediately incorporate it into their lives!

There is no wondering if they're worthy of this toy, or if others deserve it more than they do, or if they'll be good enough at playing with this toy, or whether it will fit in their toy box, or what the other kids might think of it (except perhaps how cool it is and how fun it is to play with). They may not *say* thank you right away when receiving a gift, but they definitely *show* thank you. Gratitude emits from every cell of their little bodies. They *feel* thank you in the highest, purest way, and it makes those of us providing them with their toys feel excited to shower them with more of what they want, even if they were to occasionally forget to officially thank us in words, which are a shoddy replacement for feelings anyway. (However, if we do hear or receive a sweet, heartfelt little thank-you about how much our little angel loves the toy, we cherish it and feel even more inspired to keep the toys a-comin'.)

When we are attentive to our gratitude, we raise the general daily vibration of our lives.

Gratitude is one of the most valuable tools in the energetic toolbox. When we are attentive to our gratitude, we shift out of negative moods, expand small blessings into more significant ones, and raise the general daily vibration of our lives. Gratitude makes us more compassionate, opens our hearts, and floods us with helpful energy. In business arenas, the feeling and expression of thanks helps forge and cement relationships and opportunities. It allows our work to resonate more deeply.

So other than saying thank you with more gusto as we go about our days, how can we cultivate more gratitude in our lives?

You've probably heard about gratitude journals. If you haven't ever tried one and wish to build up your allowing skills, let me encourage you—sorry, make that *beg you*—to give it a try. You will be astonished at the almost instantaneous shift in your life that takes place as you start noticing what you are thankful for on a daily basis. After all, this is just another way of saying we're going to devote our attention to that which we like ("Yes! More of this, please!") rather than that which we do not want ("Nope. Done with that. No thanks.").

Sarah Ban Breathnach created a gratitude journal movement in the nineties with her book *Simple Abundance*. She outlined a simple regimen of writing down five things for which you're thankful at the end of each day. Within weeks, she says, journalers experience less dissatisfaction and find a heightened awareness

Start a "Coolest Possible Scenarios" diary of things that might/could/would be fun to have happen.

of life's artistry and abundance. Anyone who has practiced this discipline will tell you how powerful it can be. As we go about our days, we begin looking for things to be thankful for and asking our psyches to remember what we've noted, so we can log it before bed. Contrast this with the more typical daily habits of overpacked to-do lists and fear-based stress ("If I don't remember this, *this* bad thing might happen!"), and you'll sense how valuable the shift in consciousness might be.

Perhaps you've enjoyed doing a gratitude journal in the past, but feel you'd like to try something a little different. You can access the same wonderful feelings and energy by making a positive-vibe journal of your own creation. Maybe you'd like to chronicle your "Favorite Moments of Today," reflecting back upon the day with appreciation for the experiences you most treasured. Or you might start keeping track of "What I'm Most Excited About" or "What Sounds Like *Fun,*" noting the most exhilarating possibilities in your near future.

Try a "Pray Rain Journal," where you write every day about the sensory and emotional feelings of having your desire already. The term "pray rain" comes from a Native American tradition associated with the ritual rain dance. During the dance, performers don't pray *for* rain, they pray *rain* itself. They fully engage in the feeling of experiencing the rain, the wet drops on their skin, the change in the air pressure, the color of the sky, the softness of the dampening earth under their feet. Embracing the full sensory experience of what you desire prepares you for its arrival in a visceral way, raising your energy closer to the level matching that of what you want. (People report that with pray rain journals, the object of their desire often arrives by the time they finish the notebook. My friend Jeannette[9] says to use tiny notebooks if you want it fast!)

There are so many ways to creatively log positive thoughts. Try mixing them with intentions, for instance. You could start a "Coolest Possible Scenarios" diary full of stories of things that just

9. Jeannette Maw has a great e-book about how to institute a practice of pray rain journaling. Visit her site *www.goodvibecoach.com* for more information.

might/could/would be fun to have happen. Or you could compile a "Dream List" book with categories of how you'd like to order up your preferred job/soulmate/dream house/job opportunities and anything else.

Hell, we're artists! Mix it with your media. Make little sketches of your five things, or put them to a melody, or graphically arrange the words in one of your incredibly cool layouts. Allow gratitude to infuse your art form with beauty and pleasure. Allow it to spill over into your "real work." Allow it to expand, filling your life in such a graceful way that suddenly you notice that there's no room for negative feelings—just room for what you most want.

Chapter Seven: Allowing

Allowing asks that we balance our need to give, give, give by opening our arms to receive. Let's look at where you might be unconsciously blocking some of the desires that are trying to make their way to you.

1. You're a spectacular giver. Who are the lucky recipients of your gifts? To what or whom do you give the most on a regular basis? What benefits do you receive in return? Create a visual or tactile representation of the current state of your giving and receiving, labeling your recipients. If you see a clear constriction represented in your piece, physically or visually open it up. Clip, erase, break, stretch, widen, revise—whatever it takes.

2. Do you deflect compliments or praise? If so, begin a "Just the Thanks, Ma'am" program of saying thank you and leaving it at that. No explanations, no qualifiers, no redirecting. Just say: "Thank you! Thank you very much."

3. List ten things right now, big or small, for which you're thankful.

* **Bonus Kick-Ass Challenge:** It's legend that Miss Americas maintain an impressive daily practice during the year of their crowns, writing an astonishing amount of thank-you notes—often upwards of two or three dozen a day. Okay, so you're not Miss America. Yet. You're still thankful, though, right? Who have you been meaning to thank for their help or thoughtfulness? Can you institute a regular weekly, or even daily, practice of setting aside time to thank others in writing?

Opening the Flow

Project Rec: Create a pair of Emotion Dice. Get a couple of wooden blocks that are one to two inches or larger on each side (or get crafty and make them out of another material). On each side of one block, create a representation of a desirable emotional state. Choose positive states ranging from the middle to the top of the emotional spectrum (such as hopeful, excited, joyful, or thrilled).

On the other block, depict shifts you usually find helpful and fun. Roll the dice when you want guidance with how to ascend the emotional scale and get into a better energetic place. (And do take the route we often did with the Magic Eight Ball toy of my youth. If you're not a fan of the sides that come up, just try again!)

Crazy-Easy Route: Write the word "receive" on your hand (okay, you can just put an R if you have to), and every time you look at it, say to yourself, "I receive wonderful things." Make this your default mantra all day long, and take note anytime something helpful, convenient, or delightful comes your way.

CHAPTER EIGHT

A Few Last Power Tools

You're getting the hang of it now, right? You're getting into the idea and habit of consistently nudging your energy and conscious thoughts in the exact direction of your dreams. You're learning how to deal with the dissenting and distracting voices around you (or inside you), and you're hopefully already finding that directing your focus and feelings can be useful and effective with little everyday things as well as the big artistic visions of our lives.

You've got a solid foundation for moving forward and getting those kick-ass creative projects off the ground, but just in case you need a little extra boost, here are a few more helpful tools to check out. You'll discover your own preferences for clearing energy or rounding up the troops—you probably have some in place already—but in case you'd like a few additional ideas, here are some of my favorites.

Exercises become especially helpful in the middle stages of a creative project, when resistance or fear can creep in.

Write It Out, Write Around It, Write to It

If I sense myself starting to get nervous, frustrated, or conflicted about a situation or project, I inevitably find myself turning to writing exercises. These techniques are my defaults, the places I go without even thinking about it, to find better energy.

Writing allows me to slow down and funnel the mosaic of busy thoughts into words on a page, which calms me down and forces me to choose a tack. Thoughts have a way of playing dirty sometimes, jumping forward or retreating in response to various possible solutions so I can't settle on a clear path. When I pick up one of my favorite pens[10] and begin writing, I'm able to find an eye in the storm, a quiet center from which I can unclench, witness, and make a plan.

I've journaled since about seventh grade, but found a real place for writing as an energetic application after reading *The Artist's Way* by Julia Cameron.[11] She advocates a daily writing practice, called morning pages, that I've found incredibly helpful over the years. Supersimplified, the practice asks that we write three longhand pages, first thing every morning. (Well, Julia says we're allowed to get our coffee or tea, which I appreciate.) Morning pages are meant to clear more than chronicle, so we're freed from the need to "*write* write" and can concentrate on just draining the static in our heads out onto the page where it won't interfere with our creative progress. The clarity gained from exercises like this becomes especially helpful in the middle stages of a creative project, when resistance or fear can creep in, or in between projects, as a way to casually explore the glints of inspiration that first bounce into our lives as mere possibilities.

10. For the record, I use black, micro Roller Pens by Uni-ball. I have three on my person at any given moment. It's probably not healthy, how much I love these pens.

11. Cameron, Julia. *The Artist's Way: A Spiritual Path To Higher Creativity.* New York: G. P. Putnam's Sons/Tarcher, 1992. All of Cameron's books offer incredibly valuable insights on the creative process.

I also frequently use a writing exercise I first heard attributed to John Lennon (though I can't officially confirm that). I've nicknamed it "writing around." Writing around is the process of putting a verbal spin on the nonverbal, or exporing the message of the piece in a different form. Perhaps I'm stuck on a part of a song, for instance. To *write around* it, I'd write out a page or two of paragraphs describing what the song (or this specific lyric) is really about. I'll write why sharing this particular thought matters to me, where I see the message in my own life. Usually, there's some uncertainty with the message itself that's slowing me down; taking a little time to write around it inevitably helps me get to the heart of what I really want to say. If you're stuck on a *writing* project, you can still write around it by dramatically simplifying the themes. Distill the book's message into one paragraph (making this paragraph an exercise just for you, not something you'll use officially somewhere later). Reduce each chapter's themes into a few three-word phrases. Find other ways to write about the project without writing *for* it.

Lastly, I use a technique borrowed from Gestalt psychology to write *to* a piece as if it's an entity. (Hmm, since it holds energy and vibrates, I guess it kind of is.) Try this by writing out a dialogue between you and your piece. Ask what it wants to become. Write down its response. Ask where to go next, how to solve a current conundrum. (This can be an *astonishingly* surprising and helpful exercise.) Whether the answers come from Source or your subconscious mind, you'll probably find some interesting new aspects to consider. (There's no reason you couldn't do this out loud or in your head, by the way. It's about the energy exchange, not the writing itself.)

Walking

When things get tricky, I walk. I go outside and just walk, with no headphones, route, or heart-rate monitor. The forward movement does something helpful. There's a mental unfurling as my senses

open to the sights, sounds, and scents all around. My physical energy changes. I breathe deeper and differently.

Though I live in a rugged mountain town, I'm not naturally drawn to outdoorsy or athletic pursuits. In fact, given the choice between sedentary mental engagement and a physically demanding activity, I'll pick the easy chair every time. (Maybe it's because I find internal energy so stimulating!) So walking takes some effort. I usually argue with myself at least a bit before getting out the door. But when I need it, walking is there for me, and I know I can find fresh energy and ideas when I do it.

What's a good framework for a regular walking practice? I've admired the discipline of artists like Georgia O'Keefe who took long daily walks, but I've personally been able to institute a similar practice only when living in foreign countries where a choice to drive or bike in the bedlam of local traffic would have required a death wish. So I enjoy this tool the most when it remains unstructured for me, when its free of any sense of obligation or labor. I typically go by myself, but sometimes Daisy and Mark come along. The walks might be long or short, brisk or meandering. I feel best when I'm inspired to go and just head out the door to see where my walk will lead me.

Find your own happiest way to walk—in nature, on active city sidewalks, in the morning or evening. Just enjoy the opportunity to move, and open yourself to whatever inspiration might find you. In the words of Raymond Inmon, "If you are seeking creative ideas, go out walking. Angels whisper to a man when he goes for a walk."

Clearing and Grounding

Remember discussing qi and chakras back in Chapter One? A strong, clear vibration requires smooth, flowing qi and clear bodily energy centers. We want to remove any energetic obstacles inhibiting our currents and gunking us up. Got to keep those whirling discs unclogged and sparkling, artists! The good news is we can do it quickly and by ourselves through clearing and grounding processes. I've included some specific programs here, but with your creativity, you can certainly write or imagine your own rituals. No gurus necessary—excellent!

Anytime you feel a little off or disjointed, or seem to have trouble concentrating or focusing, try one of the following exercises. You can make a big, lovely production of it or take the short and sweet route. Energy responds to our direction no matter what.

Energy responds to our direction no matter what.

Chakra Clearing

Keeping chakras clear and bright allows our bodies to serve as stronger energetic instruments. It helps us connect more easily with Source and clue in to areas where we may have energy issues taking place.

My friend Stephanie Barton came up with a great (and quick) chakra-clearing practice that she does every morning in the shower. As the water does its magic, she imagines each chakra opening up and then beautifully clearing and releasing, one by one. All unwanted or piggy-backed energy from other people swirls with the water easily down the drain to the happy energy-recycling center deep in the earth. When finished, she zips up all the open chakras, closing them to their optimal position, and says to herself, "Only love and light come into me; only love and light come out of me." Bing, bang, boom—she's ready to roll. Clearing your energy can be this quick and simple, once you know your way around your energy centers.

To help you discover more about chakras and engage more deeply in a clearing practice, I've included a full-length chakra-clearing meditation in the appendix.

Grounding

Grounding exercises help center us when we feel scattered or spacey. Taking a moment to ground your energy before a performance or meeting allows you to stand firmly in your own skin. You'll feel less vulnerable to the swaying influence of ego and fluctuating conditions, and be more relaxed and certain of your purpose.

Here are a couple ways to ground yourself.

Go outside and stand, sit, or kneel on the ground. If possible, allow part of your bare skin to come in contact with a natural surface like grass, dirt, or sand. Imagine your energy flowing down, out of the base of your spine, and reaching like roots growing deep down into the earth. Breathe. Sense the pulse of earth energy coming up into you and returning down into the earth. To take it a step further, imagine the top of your head opening up and the earth energy moving up and through you to the vastness of Source. Allow yourself to breathe deeply and find a balance between physical and spiritual energies. (See the appendix for an expanded guided grounding meditation.)

Use water. Water holds fantastic clearing, grounding, and vibration-enhancing properties. Drink plenty of water. When washing your hands or face, imagine the water clearing any negative or old energies away. Relax in a hot bath, with bath salts, if possible, for extra zing. Sit near water in nature, allowing yourself to be calmed and centered by the soothing sounds and helpful electrons of the lake, stream, or waterfall.

Lastly, you can just intend that the grounding take place, and declare that it's done. Take a deep breath and say to yourself, "My energy is clear and grounded." Most of us attach rules to energy that are similar to the rules we attach to physical matter, so a simple intention and declaration might feel insufficient to create significant results. Even though it might require a mental stretch, you can trust that energy is responsive and will follow your lead. If you feel you need to do more to see more dramatic results, go ahead and do more. If you find great results with abbreviated methods, that works too!

Your Spiritual Creative Team

I believe that we all have access to spiritual helpers. I think there may be some kind of messengers that go back and forth between Big Creative and all of us, helping inspiration find us (and helping *us* make sense of inspiration). Maybe they're muses, guides, ancestors, angels, guardians—whatever—but I think all artists benefit from the guidance and efforts of helpful spirits.

I call them my *creative team.*

To be honest, I'm not completely sure about how it all works. Sometimes my creative team feels like it might be composed of characters representing different parts of myself, my psyche; I definitely recognize shades of the chummy earth mother, the responsible firstborn, the goofball, the researcher. Other times, I feel like I'm relating with a small group of actual beings, each with defined agendas and personas.

In the end, it doesn't matter to me. I feel supported, directed, and delighted when I'm open to the guidance of my team. When I invite them into my process and daily rhythms, I feel less alone and less intimidated by the vastness and power of Big Creative. I feel like I have intermediaries—powerful, loving characters looking out for me, making sure I don't miss anything important. I'm protected and productive. I've got a *team.*

So screw it if it sounds a little nutty. It works for me. And it can work for you.

How can you get to know your creative team? How can you request and recognize their guidance?

First of all, be open to their help. Recognize the possibility of your team's existence. Go ahead and say hello, if you like. Talk to them about what's on your mind as you work on a piece or search for specific information or contacts.

Be bold and speak to them out loud, or write down your questions or messages. Many spiritual traditions insist there are two rules when working with spiritual ambassadors: (1) we must *invite* divine intervention for it to take place, and (2) there's no mind-reading allowed. So in order to keep our treasured free will up and running, apparently we've got to *ask* for help, and our requests must be *demonstrative* (spoken or written). Cover your bases. Get into the habit of *asking* your team for help anytime you'd like it, even for little things. Say your request out loud whenever you can, or jot it down somewhere.

Trust and honor the guidance you receive.

Create opportunity for connection by carving out some silence in your day.

Trust and honor the guidance you receive. Watch for it. Look. Listen. Pay special attention when something repeatedly catches your eye or crosses your mind. Take a closer look at the book that inexplicably just fell off the shelf as you walked by. Follow your sudden urge to make conversation with the person at the next table.

Establish a symbol or method of contact. I went to a Catholic high school, and we once had a visiting priest who suggested that we could create opportunities for divine messages in our lives by choosing a symbol with which God could attract our attention. I looked around that day and noticed some purple flowers on a table nearby. "Okay," I thought, "there's my symbol of divinity—purple flowers. You don't see purple flowers all the time, so that should work." I decided that when I saw purple flowers, it was a sign that I was protected and loved. Within hours, I started seeing purple flowers *everywhere.* If someone gave me flowers, they were purple. Desserts came to the table with sweet purple pansies decorating the plate. Purple hydrangea bushes lined the walkway to the home overseas where I lived as an exchange student, reassuring me just when I needed a sign that I wasn't so alone. I was even delighted to see purple wildflowers overflowing from our yard that first spring (and each one since) at the house where I now live. Yes, I acknowledge that when you're looking for something, you're more apt to find it, but over the years, purple flower appearances have gotten almost ridiculous. So now, anytime I'm craving specific guidance, I'll choose a symbol and corresponding meaning as a way to get more clarity from my intuition or inspiration.

Create opportunity for connection by carving out some silence in your day. Though it's easy to be experiencing some kind of media all the time, it feels to me that moments unencumbered by noise or information open us up most effectively for other kinds of important updates. If you're looking for guidance, consciously choose silence. Turn off the radio when you're driving. Flip off the TV while you're cooking or using it as background noise. If you're accustomed to reading whatever's nearby, put down the pamphlet/cereal box/old magazine and just sit quietly. Whatever your personal media habits, choose to just give yourself a break from them from time to time. Following a constant train of ideas takes more effort than we often realize, and stepping off the media train can bring a surprising amount of relief, along with the opportunity for clearer communication with your team.

Expect and prepare for guidance. My creative team has a way of getting active when I'm going to sleep or dreaming. Perhaps these are the times I can connect with Source with the least interference. If I'm frantically working to finish a piece and am feeling drowsy instead of motivated, I try to consider that my guides might be begging me to sleep so they can help. (And they do!) I keep a notebook by my bed to jot down the ideas that come at night, which is good, because the ideas been valuable ones, fully fleshed out and worded beautifully (even if written in sleepy, chicken-scratch handwriting). Perhaps from a place of similar experience, Saul Bellow once said, "You never have to change anything you got up in the middle of the night to write." Exactly! Try to notice patterns of heightened inspiration and equip yourself appropriately to capture fleetingly brilliant ideas.

Your Body as an Energetic Instrument

Okay, you knew this was coming. Our physical bodies serve as the primary conductor of our energy. If we fail to keep them hydrated, nourished, exercised, and rested, our energetic connection will be compromised. Maintenance matters. (It's not rocket science, either.)

You already know the basics. For highest, clearest energy, do the same things that keep your body healthy and happy in general. Drink lots of pure water. Eat whole foods. Move. Sleep. These are common-sense (and oft-quoted) recommendations for well-being, but they also have energetic underpinnings that matter to our energy work.

Water acts as an important energy conductor in our bodies. It allows the electrical impulses to flow through our cells more easily

The wisdom of our bodies tells us what we each need to do to magnify our energy and vitality. Act on it!

and keeps our elimination systems running smoothly. Many healers and psychic energy workers profess that large quantities of water are necessary to keep their personal energy clear and strong.

The food we eat contains the energy of its source, so it becomes increasingly important that we *feel good* about the soil, oceans, or pens from which it comes. (Please note that I don't define what "feeling good" means specifically in this context. A cattle rancher, organic farmer, and touring musician might have very different ideas about safe sources of their foods.) I've adopted various eating programs over the years, all of which have served me well; my only rule is to stay aligned with my consciousness. If I'm feeling like not eating meat, I don't eat meat. If I feel like eating macrobiotically, I eat macrobiotically. And when I don't feel like eating in a certain way any longer, I adjust.

Be present and listen to yourself and your body. Ayurvedic tradition tells us that the body is a genius—it reflects all the knowledge of the universe. As our bodies constantly change and adapt to our environments and demands, the individual wisdom of each of our bodies tells us what we each need to do to magnify our energy and vitality. Listen to that wisdom. Act on it!

Vigorous exercise allows us to draw from the energy around us and feel it *inside* our bodies. It's also a wonderful shifting technique, as exercise dislodges and releases sludgy energy, freeing up positive qi for our use. (In case it's not obvious, find a way to move your body that makes you grin. Loading your exercise life with *shoulds* and *have tos* is a surefire recipe for regimen abandonment.)

Rest is the most important rejuvenator of all. Some traditions hold that a part of our spirit leaves our bodies when we sleep, returning to Source to recharge and complete "upgrades" of sorts. This is why babies sleep so much, we're told. They feel unnerved in their new situation and frequently must return to the safe embrace of Source to find the strength and resolve to tackle their new environment.

If you're plagued with illness, or even just pesky (but draining) irritations like allergies or headaches, script yourself a situation where the physical problem is gone and you're delighted about it. Open yourself up to inspiration and follow up on the hits you get for approaches to resolve your issues. I tried this with seasonal allergies. Within days of my decision to be done with them, a chiropractor friend, Dr. Malin, recommended I try taking some quercetin, a vitamin C derivative available in any health-food store. It worked spectacularly, with no side effects. Your inspiration can help guide you to similar success, even in areas where you've thought you needed to live with pain, discomfort, or inconvenience.

Be good to yourself. Offer yourself the best nutrients you can find. Sleep when you need to sleep. Find a form of exercise that leaves you happy and smiling. Make your body the best instrument for energy that it can possibly be.

I hope these additional tools will help you on your way to your richest, most creative self. As we wrap up our look at energy amplifiers, we conclude part one. Next, we'll see how energy affects specific aspects of the creative process.

You're doing great. Good work, artist!

Chapter Eight: A Few More Power Tools

Each of us responds best to certain techniques and tools; it's up to us to discover which ones work most effectively in the context of our unique needs.

1. Draw/paint/represent your personal energy as a river. Commit to the metaphor. Are there any dams or eddies? Bridges? Debris? What (or whom) do these things represent in your

life? Make changes to your representation where you'd like to see them in your life.

2. Do some beginner Gestalt therapy. Put a problematic work (or any physical thing representing a current project) in a chair, sit down across from it, and have an imaginary conversation. Ask what it wants from you, what it wants to be, and what the problem or pause is about. Allow yourself to hear/absorb whatever messages come up, without judgment or opposition. Consider the new wisdom you gather (along with any surprise revelations) when you resume work on the piece.

3. Choose a special sign with which to enhance communication with your creative team. Anything that will catch your attention will work. Establish what you'd like it to mean when you see your sign. Start with simple yes-or-no symbols if you like. When driving at night sometimes, I'll sometimes say out loud, "If I see a car with a headlight out, it's a yes. Those crazy-bright HID headlights—those mean no." Then I ask questions and see what crosses my path.

* **Bonus Kick-Ass Challenge:** How do you feel about the idea of a spiritual creative team? Do you prefer the idea of working with helpers or alone? Is there anything unsettling for you about the concept of creative companions? Write a letter to your creative team that starts, "Hello, my dear Creative Team, thank you for..." If you're less certain of the idea, start your letter, "Hello, Team. If you exist, I'd like to ask..."

Opening the Flow

Project Rec: Your challenge over the next week is to give all the new tools a spin, one by one, and see how they feel for you. Each day, choose one tool: do a writing exercise, walk, ground yourself, clear your chakras, or invite your spiritual creative team to participate during a work session or any part of your life. If other ideas for working with your energy came up as you were reading this chapter, that's inspiration, baby! Try them!

Crazy-Easy Route: Try the quickie "intend and declare" method of grounding. The next time you feel a little off center or out of balance emotionally, say to yourself (out loud if possible), "I intend to be grounded and centered. My energy is balanced and clear." Imagine any unwanted energy leaving your body and only clear and bright energy remaining. Tell yourself, "It is done." And believe it.

PART TWO

Kick-Ass Creativity in Real Life

CHAPTER NINE

Kick-Ass Creativity in Action

As your energy grows and strengthens, you'll likely notice a restlessness to do something, to try something that you've been considering for awhile. You'll start getting itchy to take your newly sparkling vibes out for a spin. You'll want to get crackin' and see what all these tools can really do for you.

Well, good, 'cause the rest of our work here is *all about application.*

Theory is fabulous—hugely important for creating a solid foundation—but it won't change the state of our art or happiness *one iota* if allowed to wither in the abstract. If we wish to truly embody our most vibrant, kick-ass creative selves, we must roll up our sleeves and get our hands good and dirty. Our energy is hopefully growing clearer and brighter by the day, so let's put it to use! Let's apply it to the nuts and bolts of the creative process and really get things rolling. Yeah!

What will this mean to the bigger picture of my life?

If we were documenting your creative emergence for a television show, first we'd hear a little bit more about you, the issues or problems you'd like to solve, and your goals. The questions and exercises throughout part one hopefully helped you start to form a picture of your energy strengths, challenges, and the parts of your art and process you'd most like to enhance.

Next on the TV show we'd find out about the experts in place to guide you through your makeover journey. Oh yeah, that's *right*—you *don't* have a big crew ready to help you clean out your closets, laser your teeth to a crazy white, or psychoanalyze your whole childhood in a matter of weeks. But you do have resources just the same. We'll explore how you can get feeling great about time, money, and your current age and level of experience.

Then the show might cut to a confessional shot, where you'd report your concerns about the whole process. "Am I really ready for this?" you'd wonder aloud to the camera. "What will this mean to the bigger picture of my life? What if the changes are too hard to make, or to maintain?" Here's where our unproductive states usually come sashaying in. We've all been touched by moments of overwhelm, procrastination, and fear. We'll see ways to deal with these unwelcome diversions and move back into the flow where we belong.

You know what comes next, right? Drama! Here's where we'd see the crying, the stumbling, the ominous-looking plastic-surgery bandages. We'd see clips of shaking heads and hear mutters of, "I *quit!*" We start creating dramas like these when our creative process has some kinks. Kinks trip us up, shocking us with blocks, resistance, or dry spells, just when we were rolling along with terrific momentum. They also love to pop up when we edit, rework, and prepare to present our stuff to the world. We'll learn why kinks enter our processes, and discover ways to dissolve them, step out of their crafty traps, or just relax and wait until they lift and our focus becomes clear again.

Finally, in Chapter Thirteen, we'll ramp up to the moment of your big reveal (however this creative emergence might look for *you*). We'll address things that many of us neglect, like image, business-communication materials, and professional gear. We'll test your readiness for the thrilling big gigs of your wildest dreams. We'll go over how and where to find guidance for moving your work to the next level, no matter where you are right now. We'll even look at the wonderfully complex moments of meeting our desires up close and personally, and see how to appreciate these pinnacle moments in our creative lives with grace and full presence.

At the end of each chapter, you'll notice some "Creative Soul Search" questions. These are meant to help you uncover hidden desires and dreams, as well as areas of sticky energy, blocks, and limiting beliefs that might be affecting your creative output and fulfillment. Approach the questions by answering them in writing or through more kinesthetic forms that may appeal to you—dance your answers, draw them, vocalize them in tones, sculpt them from found objects. Use your responses to help you see new things about your creative self and the possibilities ahead.

Finally, although I'm happy to help you fill in the blanks here and there, I know that *you* already know your personal creative process better than anyone. You know where your energy tends to jump or soar or skip with delight. You also probably know where your energy occasionally falters or gets a little gummy on you. Hopefully, with a few of the following tweaks and approaches, you'll soon find yourself blowing right past those old trouble spots and having *more fun* creating *better work* than ever before.

Now let's go play with all our fun new toys.

CHAPTER TEN

Resources

We draw strength and capability from our resources. Time, money, age and experience—we crave the perfect alchemy of these elements as we bring inspiration into form. Can we ever have enough time? How can we find the funds to create the impact we desire? Can we trust that our present age and experience are exactly right for where we are in our creative journeys? If you've felt that the resources you need have been elusive (or nonexistent), here you'll find ideas for seeing situations in new ways and scripting better outcomes. Let's get you feeling supported, baby!

The Resource of Time

Ooohhhhh, time.

Time may matter most when we don't feel we have any of it available to us, but it also starts feeling significant when we're on a deadline, when we feel the pinch on our other

resources, or even when we catch a glimpse of our maturing appearance in an unexpected mirror.

Time stands up for our notice in other ways, too. We celebrate perfect timing (or worry that we've missed the mark). We fantasize about big, open, free expanses of it (days and days to do nothing but create!). We note the ages of our heroes and peers, mercilessly comparing our paths to their progress. In our best moments, we lose track of time as we leap with full engagement into the flow of our work.

You *can* find the time you need. Your art and spirit depend on it.

We feel and recognize time's power. We know we must reconcile ourselves to the fact that it's part of our creative terrain. So how do we balance the demands of busy lives with the call to devote *time* to our creative passions? How do we quiet the ticking clock without losing touch with the other valid demands in our lives?

Are we kidding ourselves? Is there *really* enough time to do it all?

My friend Zafod, an inventor and sculptor, says, "You can do anything, but you can't do everything." Without the relentless pressure of time, I suspect we might indeed take on the widest expanse of possibility, even to our own detriment. Time keeps us real, pointedly requiring that we make choices.

If you're feeling crunched for creative time, as most of us do (at least a little), it's time to open things up. There are tons of books and programs, even digital devices, out there to help you manage the tasks and commitments in your life, but if those aren't doing the trick, some new approaches are probably in order.

You *can* find the time you need, through both energetic methods and practical adjustments in daily habits. Your art and spirit depend on it.

Your Free Time Revolution: Getting Clear, Real, and Creative

If you really want more time for yourself and your creative work, start by figuring out exactly what more time means for you.

Let's Get Clear.

What kind of time do you want? Would you like an hour or two each day to work on your project? Do you crave more extensive periods of time—six or seven hours at a crack—to really delve in? Are you a serial project completer, working on one project at a time until it's done, or do you take more of a mosaic approach, keeping several pieces in active stages at any given time? When you find yourself in a moment of great creative output, notice what kind of time it took to arrive there. Was it quicker than you imagined? Longer? What other elements contributed to your state of productivity? Be honest with yourself. How do you work best? What do you really want? Be clear.

Say no to *everything* that doesn't absolutely energize, delight, or relieve you in some way.

Once you've defined what you'd like to experience timewise, begin applying finale thinking: *put yourself mentally into the position of already having the situation you want.* Feel the situation as if you're in it already, and then allow yourself (or the powers-that-be) to start creating the environment for it to exist.

If other commitments are an issue (family responsibilities, work schedules, community demands), imagine that you're just received a phone call that has let you off the hook for a commitment you find draining or overly time-consuming. Feel the relief of suddenly open time, the sense of freedom and lightness that an unexpected space in your schedule can create. Or imagine yourself telling a friend how amazing it's been since you've had ________ (whatever or whomever that might be) freeing up all that time. As you become adept at appreciating open time on a consistent basis, you'll find gifts of time actually dropping into your lap. Allow yourself to *accept these gifts* and use them for your creative work.

An important component of jumpstarting a free-time revolution for yourself is to start saying no to *everything* that doesn't absolutely energize, delight, or relieve you in some way. Making a living and caring for our surroundings and families are activities worthy of our devotion and time, but let's face it, they don't end there. We all get roped into a lot more activities than might be required by our lives' general task descriptions.

You're going on an energy diet, and the big drainers have to go.

If it helps, tell yourself that just for a finite amount of time—say, the next three months—you're going to pare down dramatically. You're going on an energy diet, and the big drainers have to go. Only the most delicious, nourishing stuff for you. Yes, you'll keep up the essentials, but you're going to opt out of being the hero of the bake sale, intramural league, carpooling gang, book club, recycling committee, or sports night for a while. You're going to let the machine pick up more often, and miss a couple boring barbeques to which you'd normally say yes out of a sense of obligation. Your neighbors might not have homemade May Day baskets this year (unless that's your creative thing!), but I promise you, they'll get over it.

Another task to help you find fresh available time will be keeping a weeklong, running log of where your time is actually going. Most digital and online planners allow you to print out daily schedules. Print out seven blank days (or just use blank sheets of paper, if you like) and for one week keep track of where your hours really go. You may discover that you engage in a lot more time-sucking activities than you think. These can include Web surfing, watching TV, flipping through magazines, or making a bigger deal out of household or work tasks than is necessary. There is typically a lot more time in our days than we believe is available, but we tell ourselves that we *need to do* certain activities for a specific reason: to relax, to unwind, to keep up with trends, to know what's happening in the world, to escape.

Try this: start by taking fifteen minutes a day that you are spending on a nonessential activity and putting it toward your creative passion. If your fifteen-minute chunk happens to turn into something more substantial and exciting, well that's just dandy! But the fifteen minutes is enough to do the job. If you feel really pressed for time, set a timer and go ahead and stop when it goes off.

Use the time however you like. Draw, paint, dance, write, or design. Sit in a chair and *think* about doing one of those things. Putter around the garage and find the tools you've been missing. Write a charming note to someone in your field. Just start getting *back in the game.* Begin letting your art penetrate the radar of your daily rhythms again.

You'll find the fifteen-minute regimen effective because it's low stress. We can get ourselves to do fifteen minutes of almost anything without creating too much resistance. And before you know it, you'll be developing a habit of (1) watching for opportunities to work/create, and (2) honoring those urges and opportunities with *action.* Even if your actions are small, they still represent *forward movement.* They'll get you back into the groove.

You'll feel more engaged with your work, more aware of it in the other parts of your life. And you'll find that the payoffs far exceed your sacrifices; you'll be more relaxed (since you won't be worrying that life is passing you by), you'll be less stressed (because you're in flow and energizing yourself more consistently), your own personal world will be more interesting than the gloom and doom that sells news airtime, and you won't need to escape your reality (because it'll be much more interesting!).

By letting go of the *how,* the precise way we'd prefer help to arrive, we might see that help is already here.

Begin accepting support. *Allow* more time to find its way into your life. If you tend to deflect offers and gestures of support, practice saying things like, "Really? Thank you! Let's set a time. I'd love that." And do it. Too often we are surrounded by people who truly want to help, but we dismiss their offers, deciding that the support we crave needs to come in a certain form or from a specific person.

By letting go of the *how,* the precise way we'd prefer help to arrive, we might see that help is already here. Perhaps your company has a split-time program in which you could work at home for a portion of your week, saving you a hefty commute (oh, but you're worried that it might be hard to concentrate out of the office). Or the Mary Poppinsesque nanny you imagine hasn't yet arrived on the scene, but you have a neighbor who keeps mentioning she's be happy to watch your little one sometime (hmm, but you're not sure if she's serious). Or your spouse mentions that if you really wanted it, that attic space could probably be reworked into a room for you to work (shoot, yeah, but you're not sure if it would be worth the hassle and expense).

Accepting support will probably require releasing a martyr persona. Yep, it's hard to hold on to victimhood when people are helping you all over the place. I guess you'll have to just get used to the idea that you're meant to create, and now's the time for you to move forward.

Let's Get Real.

Release some of the ideas you might have about having everything perfect before you can really do anything. We live in a different world than the masters of the past; we are more susceptible to interruption and communications than any generation before. Well, so it is. This is our life. These are our times. (And sometimes the same rascals that bug us these days—cell phones, email—save us massive amounts of time in ways we no longer even notice).

Rituals are great—they can be very helpful—but keep them short.

So every single thing on our to-do lists might not be completed before we begin that magnum opus. So our homes aren't as sparkling as our mothers might have been able to keep them (in a time of different expectations, different dreams, and different cultural roles). So we're working in forty-five-minute chunks rather than the four-hour ones we'd prefer (or think we'd prefer). So we have other jobs and responsibilities to attend to beyond our creative passion. And maybe we occasionally work at the kitchen table or in the basement or garage instead of the buzzing cafes, well-equipped workshops, or serene libraries we'd rather haunt. It's okay. In every time, every generation, there have been challenges. (How about the Plague? That must have been a big one!) Still, great art and innovation take place. Whatever our supposed limitations and frustrations, let's just get on with it and work anyway.

Next, ditch the long, drawn-out readiness rituals. Rituals are great—they can be very helpful—but keep them short. Maybe two minutes of deep breathing would help you get into the vibe *almost* as well as a half-hour meditation before each work session. Maybe a few longhand pages will help you clear your mind as well as the in-depth journaling you've done in the past. You want ritual? Light a candle and voilà! You've got instant atmosphere and connection (if that's what you intend). Do what you need to do, but be conscious about how much time and effort you need to devote to the process of readying yourself. It's a thin line between preparation and procrastination. Just enough is enough.

Let's Get Creative.

Our creativity itself serves us as we seek solutions to the inconveniences that surface in our work rhythms and environments. Get out of victim/helpless mode and into what-might-work mode.

There are always ways to take control of our challenges and step into a more empowered, capable state of mind. Maybe a white-noise generator, headphones, or some classical music and a shut door will be more effective than getting your family (or neighbors, or animals, or traffic) to remain absolutely silent as you try to concentrate. Perhaps the extra hour or two of sleep you thought critical to your sanity can be sacrificed more easily than you imagined for some—also sanity enhancing—open time to work each day. Or maybe the long commute to work can be put to good use with a voice recorder for getting down ideas, or with audio programs about technique or your market. If your location allows, you could even take the train instead of the car for extra time to think or write or sketch.

Consider implementing a weekly work night when you are officially off-duty from home and family responsibilities. Quell protests by easing into the transition and setting up the situation for least resistance. (For instance, leave dinner in the fridge if you're the usual cook; choose low-conflict nights if your family has sports, lessons, or other activities to work around; and make your work night coordinate with your "other work" schedules). Or how about initiating a creative co-op? Do you have friends who would like to find more time for their projects too? Perhaps you can pool your resources and give one afternoon or evening a month in exchange for three or four other free ones.

Be bold! Be open to inspiration! If one or more of the ideas above sounds like a plan that might work for you (or if it spurred you to think of a great one of your own), go ahead and try it. Get that momentum going and allow the universe to expand on your own steps forward.

What's your story? What needs to change to make you feel great about the age you are right now?

The Resources of Age and Experience

It's our *age*. It's not the work, timing, or anything else. We're sure of it. *Our age is the real issue.*

It's easy to get tangled up in concerns about age. We imagine that our years are somehow misaligned with our abilities or desires. We're certain that *if only we could shift a few years a different direction*, things would be entirely different.

The window of perfect timing can feel incredibly narrow when it comes to age. We're too young to be taken seriously. We're too old to accomplish what we really want to do. The market's all about experience until we're wise and mature, and then, suddenly, the cult of youth is back in fashion.

To be fair, in some fields there *is* an element of age awareness, but most of the time, gifted creators of any age will find a home for their work. Besides, by now we know that we all actively participate in attracting whatever we experience.

So where are you in the age game? What's your story? Is your story supporting your desires or holding you back? What needs to change to make you feel great about the age you are right now?

Young 'Uns

Maybe you're just out of school or just getting started. You have little to show in way of experience or resume. You have the energy and excitement to do great things, but feel your lack of connections and resources or who knows what else holds you back. You might find yourself reporting how "hard it is to get a break," how "tough it is to get any respect for my ideas," or how "there's too much to do just managing life—paying rent, dealing with housemates, etc—to get anything significant done."

Transform your story into a more powerful one. Take full inventory of your situation and then put increasingly more attention on the parts that are working positively for you. For instance, you might note, "It does feel great to have only myself to be responsible for right now," or "My current gig isn't a career, but I don't have to take it home with me. I love that I can put my full attention on my pieces."

Maybe you'll discover other benefits of the moment, like, "I love the sense of synergy I feel with my roommates. Everyone always seems to be doing something creative and cool," or, "I'm so impressed by my friends lately. I feel so hopeful and excited for them, and for me, as we all make such great progress." It might even be about the work itself, as in, "It's freeing to feel like I can go any direction I want with this collection. I'm so glad I'm not tied into any particular style. The only person with expectations for my work is me."

MIDDLIN'

Maybe you're not an artistic freshman anymore. Perhaps you're smack in the middle of your journey, having done a few exciting things, but with bigger ideas for the projects ahead. Middle age is gaining on you, and you're developing angst about it.

You're looking—and feeling—tired. You handle a full plate of responsibilities from dawn until bedtime. Your life is loaded with the demands of relationships, mortgages, children and their activities, "real" jobs, car payments, school costs, managing a household, aging parents, and who knows what else.

You already know that singing the "I'm-so-busy" song won't get you where you want to go. Well, sorry to share the bad news, but you also won't get the goods by lamenting that you're "withering away, with no time to work," "feeling drained from always doing things for everybody else!" or "just wishing there were more energy for what I really want to do."

Perhaps your age concerns center more on conflicts about timing major life steps or gauging your artistic impact. "I want to have a baby," you think, "but I only have a few good dancing years left." Or, "I wanted to write the great American novel before I was thirty, and now it looks like I'll be fifty! What happened to my drive? Where the hell is my ambition?" You might worry that your best work is behind you, thinking, "I'm over. I don't have a cutting edge bone in my body anymore. What will I do now?"

What would be a more empowering view of the situation? What *do* you have? You probably have a lot of *content* happening around you—the stories of middle life are full of understated drama. You are a close witness to dozens of rich characters and crises; the stakes can feel quite high every day for those around you (or even for you yourself). Maybe your mantra could be, "Boy, I have so much material to draw from right now." And maybe your approach will be, "Jot it down. Get the gist, and just jot it down." Keep a journal with little snippets of possibility; release yourself from the idea that each thought needs to be fully realized in order to hold space in your creative life. Or email yourself the little ideas and keep them in one folder for future review. You can expand on them when you have a moment, perhaps sometime down the road when that blank page is staring back at you with expectation.

Maybe you can focus on how well you're actually using your available time and energy. If you rarely procrastinate—because you *can't*—you can note with a satisfied nod, "Wow, I never thought I'd be so effective with little pockets of time." I love this one, because it's *so true*. Our use of resources tends to expand to whatever we feel we have available to us. Unchecked, we'll spend whatever money we make, book up all our free time with activities and leisure, allow our brand new shelves to fill right up with stuff. Being conscious of limitations in a positive way can help us make decisions. So highlight the positive nature in your life's parameters. Try, "I'm still working, still creating, even while managing a lot of other things in my life really well. I'm keeping the pump primed."

And you surely are.

Wise and Willin'

Perhaps you're on the other end of the spectrum, wondering if your *maturity* keeps you from being as cutting edge or energetic (or anything else) as you'd like. Maybe you feel like your creative market caters to the youthful and prefers their art suppliers to be that way, too. These days you've been a *Ma'am* or *Sir* for longer than you were a *Miss* or *Young Buck*, and so you worry that your window of opportunity has passed.

What's your age story? Do you ever say things like, "Well, at my age it doesn't make sense to _____." Or, "I wish I would have learned to play the guitar (or sculpt, paint, dance, write short stories, cook) when I was younger" (as if your life and learning capacities are now over).

How about adopting a more positive, powerful statement like, "Well, at my age, I finally know what I want to do, which is great!" Or, "At my age, I'm certainly over feeling self-conscious about trying new things the way I did when I was a teenager." Or try this: "At my age, thank goodness I don't have to ask anyone's permission anymore. What a freedom that is!"

Use the pressure of age to move you forward instead of hold you back.

As you consider learning a new skill, use the pressure of age to move you forward instead of hold you back. Incorporate it into a declaration, such as, "I'm going to be a year older next year whether I take piano lessons or not, so I might as well give it a try." Move your focus to areas where you have power and capabilities. Maybe it's something like, "My parents couldn't afford to send me to art classes, but I have the money myself to do it now. I'm so glad to finally get the chance to do it after all these years of wanting to try." Or, "Waiting this long has given me lots of time to get ready. I've got a lot of built-up energy to put into it!" Or, "I finally have a sense of myself and my life experience that makes me feel qualified to _______. People my age are a hugely growing market, and I could represent their point of view."

The Resource of Money

Selling out. Going "commercial." Money gets a bad rap in the creative community sometimes. There's *nothing* wrong with money, or even with wanting it, enjoying it, or acquiring it to do the things we desire. *Money is simply energy.* It's desire in action—energetic potential pinging around from person to person as we trade the value of something we have (or are willing to do) for something we *want.*

Money represents options. When it's plentiful, our sense of possibility expands, and we feel able, generous, powerful. When

See money as a lifelong character in your experience. If you don't love your money messages, what would you rather they say?

it's scarce—or when we sense future scarcity—our valve constricts, and we feel limited, stuck.

If money has been an issue for you, do a little digging about your internal money messages. Spend some time journaling on the following questions:

- What was the vibe around money in your household growing up? (For example: "Don't worry about it. It's taken care of," or "There's never enough!")
- What are the earliest feelings you can recall having about money?
- What might your family's money vibe and your early recollections reveal or explain about your current relationship with money?
- Describe your relationship with money as if it's a person you know. How close are you? How often do you see each other? How do you feel about each other?
- Do you worry about bad things happening in your life if you were to make a lot of money? Would this change if you inherited or won the money versus earning it?
- Do you feel your relationships would change if you had a lot of money? How so?

These questions ask that we see money as a lifelong character in our experience. Its influence reaches way back into our childhoods and pulls up a chair at the table of our relationships, work, and adult identities. If you don't love your money messages, what would you rather they say? What's your ideal money vibe?

Financial Backstory

Most of us have a love-hate relationship with money. We love the rich sense of potential it gives us, but worry that its power would demand things of us we may not wish to give. (Fame holds the same duality, by the way.) We worry about all kinds of situations—

the kids turning to sex and drugs, an expectation of increasingly better work from us, our friends deciding we're *different*, money-grubbing relatives coming out of the woodwork, upsetting the delicate power structure with our mate, awkwardness with picking up the tab. It doesn't matter what the fears are, just that they exist in our money vibe. Our concerns might be practical or ridiculous, but if they continually arise, they're constricting the flow of money into our lives. They create *energetic tethers* that hold us down and keep us from reaching our true heights.

Use your tools to dissolve your money gunk. Do a flipping list: write out everything you *don't want* to happen, and flip these into positive desires by counter each entry with a better, positive result. Refuse to allow yourself to indulge in negative money fantasies, whether they're dramatic (your you-as-a-bag-lady fixation) or minor (your anxiety at the thought of giving up your supertechie PDA phone). Use your favorite shifting mechanisms to get you out of the hot zone and into a neutral or positive place, and then create new money scripts representing how you'd like to feel about your financial picture.

Find the lighter side of things; play happy little money games with yourself. Imagine that you've tapped into a universal "multiplied rebate program." For every dollar you spend, intend and expect that ten additional dollars are coming back to you in some lovely way. Do this as you complete transactions all through your day.

Expand on the prosperity you *do* have through appreciation. Are you healthy? Is your home warm and comforting? Do you have an abundance of great, supportive friends? Are your cupboards full of groceries? My mom recently told me a story about how when she was a young mother with a growing family, she'd remarked to my grandma about what a chore it was to carry in all the heavy bags of groceries. Grandma smiled, surprised, and recalled that carrying groceries had been her favorite household task, because whenever there were lots of groceries, it meant they were doing all right, and she'd be able to feed their big family well. My mom said she never forgot Grandma's response and never again complained about bringing in the groceries. And now I better appreciate how

my grandmother attracted the resources to keep her family fed (and her spirits up) during those tough times when she was a widowed mother of eight.

No Sighs, Just Whys (Altogether Now)

Start a money-meeting group with some friends who also want to pump up their income.

We create the strongest, most magnetic money vibe when we pair our desire for more money with a healthy dose of *why*. If you had a ton of money—whatever "a ton" means for you—how would you use it? How would it really affect your life and art on a daily basis?

When we get certain about why we want more money, we begin dropping into the feeling state of our wants almost instantaneously. Group energy can be helpful too. In her terrific book *Wishcraft*,[12] Barbara Sher writes about women's empowerment groups and how structuring some regular support can spur great ideas and energy. Try it for yourself; start a money-meeting group with some friends who also want to pump up their income. Take turns sharing the following:

- How much money you'd like to attract into your life right now (Be specific. You may add the phrase "or more" to the end of your amount, but just saying "as much money as possible" doesn't cut it.)
- Why you want it
- How *exactly* you'd use it
- How you'd feel if you were able to do these things
- What positive changes you'd feel in your life
- Three ways—imaginative or actually pending—that this money could quickly appear in your life
- Three things you're thankful for regarding your current money situation

12. Sher, Barbara, with Annie Gottlieb. *Wishcraft: How to Get What You Really Want*. Chicago: Ballantine Books, 1996.

Allow each person to speak, uninterrupted, for a set amount of time—say seven or eight minutes. (Being able to speak freely without interruption is an energy-opening exercise in itself—it feels so good to be heard!) After the allotted minutes, open the floor to questions, exploration, suggestions, inspiration, sharing of resources, and encouragement. A few other rules to observe: *no* amount or plan is to be disparaged, no matter how far out it might seem. Honor each other by seeing possibilities instead of limitations. Each person should set one action-based goal to complete before the next meeting (or before an email or phone check-in at a later date). Give follow-up reports at the next meeting to chart positive progress and efforts (not to ruminate on what's *not working*).

You'll want to choose people whom you like and trust, of course, but they needn't be your best friends. Allow yourself to choose individuals with whom you can create a new template of yourself.

You can form these kinds of groups for any purpose—creative projects, career goals, even finding a soulmate. I had one a few years ago in which we collectively repaired a bad credit rating, laid the groundwork for a children's portrait business, finished a book, instituted an exercise regimen, and embarked on a new career as an art teacher. Lest you think this kind of thing is only for chatty women, my husband Mark (a professional photographer) has started three of these groups in the last few years. He's combined complimentary creative professionals from the fields of photography, graphic design, writing, advertising, and public relations to share ideas, deal with challenges, and create synergy. It's been a fantastically successful enterprise for all the participants involved.

Creative Accounting

Here's another way to have some fun with finances: start a Divine Debit Account.

Find an old unused check register and create an imaginary account—your DDA, if you like. Start off with a balance high

enough to pay off any outstanding debts—the credit cards, mortgage, student loans, car, and anything else.

Write in the *actual, exact amount* needed to pay off each creditor. This step sounds like a hassle, but it's important. Many times, those of us with a sludgy money flow have only a vague idea of what we really have and what we really owe.[13] (Back in the day, I felt that I was doing fine with an intuitive approach to my checking-account balance. I racked up $1,000 in overdrawn bank fees in one year.) Getting honest—and precise—with yourself here will dissolve niggling little anxieties you aren't even aware of, I promise.

Now once your debts are "paid in full," it's time to have some fun. For the next thirty days (or longer, if you're having a really good time) give yourself a hefty sum—say, ten thousand dollars—to spend from your DDA account every day.[14] Every day when you wake up, imagine how you'll spend your ten thousand dollars today and write down the expenditures in your register.

This exercise brings up fantastic insights as to what we really think we need to be happy and how much money those things will require. You may even discover that your deepest desires are unrelated to things one can purchase.

Have *fun* with this! What kind of adventures would you have? How much money does it take to make you feel secure? What kind of fun gifts would you give? Whom would you help? Where would you travel? Would you support (or start) a charity or nonprofit? Would you move? Would you change your job? What kind of materials, instruments, facilities, or staff might you bring into your creative work?

Use the clues to help you see what fun little desires might be lurking around under the surface. There are wonderful hints of

13. Consider entering info for all your accounts onto a secure website such as *www.mint.com,* which provides a synchronized, summarized up-to-date snapshot of your complete financial picture. Mint.com happens to be free, so you have no excuse!

14. Parts of this practice were inspired by the Checkbook exercise in the Abraham-Hicks book, *Ask and It Is Given.*

future desires and projects that emerge when we're freed from monetary constrictions.

Show Me the Money—the Actual Money

Sure, we're happy to receive new *opportunities* for making money. If we put out the word and the universe presents us with new gig ideas or the discovery of something we can sell, we'll take it. But sometimes, it's really about the cold, hard, green stuff. There's nothing wrong with asking for universal abundance to show itself in the form of good old *cash.*

If this is the case, create a script for having the cash you want. Imagine how you'll feel—the relief, delight, satisfaction—when putting your cash to its intended use. Imagine the bank cashier's impressed expression at the large amount of your deposit; visualize the numbers you want to see on the bank receipt. See the wad of cash in your wallet or purse, if that makes you feel good. Feel the skip in your step after you've paid off a loan balance in full. Feel the excitement as you use your new equipment, drive your new vehicle, or open the door to your new studio, if that's what the cash has provided.

Put your quiet times or creative meditations to work for your financial health.

Put your quiet times or creative meditations to work for your financial health. Imagine a huge, spinning vortex of hundred dollar bills all funneling down into you and your life. Or tell yourself first thing in the morning that for the whole day ahead, you are a *money magnet:* you'll receive money in fun ways all day long. In your journal, stoke possibility by coming up with at least three fab scenarios as to how the money could drop into your lap almost immediately. Make them as fanciful as you wish.

Artistic Tithing

The Bible mentions a religious practice called *tithing* that's still observed in some spiritual traditions. It asks that ten percent of one's income be given directly to his or her church or spiritual organization. Now this is ten percent off one's whole income, not ten percent of "whatever's left." This is no clinking change in the barista's jar; it's a substantial sum (and commitment). We're in a time of

tight margins, I know. I can hear your groans from here as you imagine giving up ten percent of your income (for anything).

Tithing makes a lot of sense to me, however, in the context of Source energy. When someone commits to devoting a sizable portion of income to their spiritual community, they're making a show of faith that they believe in the universal Source. They're trusting that there's plenty to go around, that the universal laws of expansion and increase will return it to them, perhaps many times over. They're showing that they're not buying what all the gloom-and-doom financial forecasts are selling. They're choosing to believe that *there is enough*.

Trust that there's plenty to go around, that the universal laws of expansion and increase will return it many times over.

How many of us could benefit from a similar faith about our work? As mentioned in the earlier section about time, perhaps our tithing could be in *hours*. (I'll be reasonable—make that ten percent of waking, non-working hours.) Or maybe we could tithe our *nurturing energy and actions*. For each nine things we do for others, we'd commit to one act of kindness and nurturing for ourselves. Maybe it's back to *money*; think of the gear/toys/supplies/resources we could enjoy if ten percent of our total income were going right back into the activities we find most rejuvenating and thrilling! There are dozens of ways to use this technique to make a show of faith about the importance and value of your work.

The key is to tap into the abundance that is truly available to us. Believing in the prosperity of Source—whether in terms of money, time, energy, inspiration, friendship, support, or opportunities—makes it stronger and more palpable in our daily lives. It may be that you're a natural in one area (say, time) and you struggle in another (perhaps money). You'll probably have a sense of whether you'd like to expand a strong area first or strengthen a weaker spot, but either way, you'll find yourself with a richness and fullness in your tithe area as you begin to expect and believe in the returns that tithing brings.

There is a caveat here. Conviction in the value of tithing and belief in its rewards will set up a terrific sense of expectation that will serve you beautifully as your creativity begins taking off. However, stressed-out vibes full of concern and impatience, with messages of "It's not working! Why isn't it working?!" will do just the opposite. Feel your way to the protected, abundant, inspired self you know is your most natural state of being, and honor the journey by listening to your instincts as you go.

Creative Soul Search

The perfect age to be for what I do (or would like to do) is ______
because ______

My age and experience are perfect for what I want to do because ______

If I could go back in time and had the resources, I'd have studied ______

If I absolutely had to, I could learn this now by ______

I could really go after my creative dream if I had ______

I could probably have this if I tried ______

or asked ______
or stopped ______
or believed ______

I'm really thankful for ________________________________

____

____

I thought my creative frustration was due to ____________

____

____

But I think it might actually be more about _____________

____

____

I might be able to find fifteen extra minutes a day if I _____

____

____

CHAPTER ELEVEN

Unproductive States

When we're caught up in an unproductive state, we're just that: not producing. Our inspiration is thwarted, our resolve is weak. We're sorry excuses for the vibrant creators we know we can be. What greases the wheels for these slides into frustration? What can we do to sidestep the negative spirals and annoying detours? Is it possible to live the creative life without occasionally touching down into these minefields? Let's see.

Unproductive State of Overwhelm

Yeah, yeah, I know, we're all *overwhelmed.* If I hear one more person, including me, talk about how overwhelming life is, I'm going to throw up.

Discussing our state of overwhelm has become a popular pastime.

By changing our language, we change the results we see in various life situations.

It's an epidemic. We're overwhelmed with opportunities, responsibilities, and possibilities. We face an unbelievable array of choices every day. We consume and commit to too much. Media deftly convinces us that we want to do everything, have everything, and be everything—and ridiculously, *we believe it!* Discussing our state of overwhelm has even become a popular pastime. Maybe we think that disclosing it excuses the stressed-out vibes we're giving off (or somehow shows what admirable little troopers we are).

We can step back from the brink of overwhelm by treating it like the unwelcome feeling state that it is. We can use self-care shifts and breathing exercises to slow down and see our situation with new eyes. We can remind ourselves that we're already, always, where we need to be and doing what we need to do. We can choose to *opt out* of anything that doesn't make us sing with delight.

I'd also like you to try something new: I want you to become much more aware of how you're *speaking* about being overwhelmed in your daily life and creative work. Using some neuro-linguistic programming processes (NLP, for short) can help shift us out of any unproductive patterns with impressively rich results. An interesting aspect of NLP centers on something called *transformational grammar*—that is, how your language choices reflect (and affect) your life. This theory asserts that by changing our language, we change the results we see in various life situations.

So if feeling swamped is an issue for you, remove any term similar to *overwhelmed* (like *so busy, crazy,* or *hectic*) from your linguistic repertoire. Act as if these words (and preferably concepts) no longer exist for you. From now on, you're going to focus on the pockets of freedom and time you *do* have. You'll note the ways you feel effective and able, rather than at your wit's end. If you've heard yourself say things like "I just don't have any time for me anymore" or "Real life just makes it impossible to focus on my creative work," it's definitely time for an adjustment. Replace disempowering habitual sayings with a mantra that is true but neutral, or that is more reflective of what you want. Try something like, "I'm actually doing okay," for a start. Or maybe, "I seem to find a little more free time every day," or "This is cool. Things are running more smoothly all the time. I feel like everything's opening up."

Affirmations, mantras, and other conscious speaking choices work most effectively when they are stated in positive terms and when they are *true at some level*, even a very small one. Thus, you'll want to avoid words like *don't, not,* and *never* in your statement, and be sure that the statement is authentic for you. You're not trying to convince yourself of something that's untrue: you're merely *reminding* yourself of a truth that you might sometimes forget. A statement like "I have plenty of time every day for what's most important to me" can be great for helping us remain aligned to the faith that *all is unfolding exactly as it should* or some other helpful tenet of our personal belief system.

Resist the urge to conversationally compete for the prize for *most overwhelmed* or *busiest by far*. It's tremendously fashionable to report, in great detail, all the consuming activities and responsibilities we manage in our busy modern worlds. Listen respectfully, if you like (internal eye-rolling is acceptable), but refuse to join in as peers compare notes on all the very valid reasons that they can't pursue whatever they most desire (such as travel, creative projects, a new business). You know better.

It's not being Pollyannaish or disingenuous to direct conversations toward what's working, rather than what's not; it's choosing the part of the story you wish to tell. It's reaching toward inspiration rather than bonding over the status quo. The more we tell a particular story, the more it becomes true for us. So if you allow the fun, lively, exciting parts of your creative journey to float to the surface of conversations, those parts grow energetically, actually becoming *more true* as they slowly edge out the negative sides of our stories.

Talking Yourself Into Balance

Maybe you're concerned about how to allot your efforts among life's various demands. With so many options for how to spend your days, it's easy to feel you're missing out on one aspect of life as you try to pursue another.

When I began singing a lot in my early twenties, I frequently found that gigs interfered with social opportunities. Most weekend evenings, I was booked to play in clubs or for private parties, so

Creators' minds often process in mosaic-like (rather than linear) patterns.

I found myself having to decline (really appealing) invitations. "I can't," I'd say. "I have to sing." When I started being more aware of my language, I realized that a change was in order. I really *liked* singing. I felt lucky to be doing it for a living, and I was still able to attend most social gatherings, even if I were late. So I made a conscious change in the way I talked about my gigs.

I decided I'd no longer even vaguely hint that my work was some kind of obligation or chore—no more *can'ts* or *have tos.* I would start my adjustment by speaking neutrally and matter-of-factly about music jobs. When invited to a fun event, I'd smile and warmly say, "Oh! I'm singing that night. Could I come by afterwards?" The change was almost immediate in people's responses. People started reacting with a respectful, "Oh! That's so cool!" or, "Oh, wow, that's right! Maybe we could come by for a drink before the party and listen to you for a set."

Just a simple shift in language began literally bringing the party to me, removing any conflict I felt about missing out by choosing to devote time to my art and career.

Emergency Action Plan for the Overwhelmed

I know there are some of you in sticky situations right this moment. Maybe you're even thinking: "Okay, okay, I'll stop talking about it in the long-term, but what else can I do *today?!*"

Take out a piece of paper and start listing all the things on your mind. Whatever it is that you feel you have to do, be, remember, or take care of—all of it—needs to get on this list. It will probably take you about twenty minutes to get most of it written down. Go ahead and continue to add on stragglers as you think of them.

Sometimes, believe it or not, this *one action*—dumping our busy minds out on the page—can be enough to calm us down and help us find a direction.

A big part of overwhelm originates from the sense that *everything* in our lives feels like an absolute top priority. Creators' minds often process in mosaic-like (rather than linear) patterns; we have a special talent for finding metaphors and subtle relationships, finding connections between seemingly disparate concepts. This ability helps us in our work, and I suspect it's the reason creative people are often seen as messy types. Many of us prefer to have everything visible and spread out around us to encourage this mosaic-type mental processing. It all makes perfect sense to *us*. Mosaic processing can be effective with physical elements, but when we apply this "keep everything on top" style to managing what's on our *minds*, we get overwhelmed. We can't give equal, immediate attention and effort to everything on our lists. It's *not possible*. And it'll make you nuts.

So, my little overwhelmed one, you're going to get your list going and then look at it with new eyes. You're going to divide it into five areas—A, E, I, O, U:

Actions: tasks we know how to do and can do now if necessary. (For example, do taxes. Sign and return contract. Back up computer.)

Emotional concerns: worries we hesitate to consciously address or cannot resolve directly. (Is R mad at me? Is K's school a good fit for her? Is my new show any good? Will my sister be okay?)

Implementations: tasks providing long-term value and well-being, usually requiring a regular disciplined effort of some kind; these can be easily put off, but are important for a strong foundation. (Get in better shape. Practice more. Organize office.)

Obstructions: nitpicky tasks and issues that bug us and cause overly dramatic sighs when we realize we *still* haven't done them! (Do the dishes in the sink. Get gas. Mail out orders.)

Uncertainties: action tasks with missing info. (Call guy about studio space—what's his name? Book violinist or violist—which? Enter contest if I can decide which recipes to include in application.)

Our biggest stressors show up in two areas: *actions* and *uncertainties*.

Start by just choosing three things that *you feel like doing*.

Most of the time the things our biggest stressors show up in two areas: *actions* and *uncertainties*. When one or both of these lists get too large, our vibe starts getting cloudy and heavy. That's when our *emotional* and *implementation concerns* jump in; how could they possibly resist such deliciously gloomy, sticky energy? Finally, we become walking time bombs, looking for something, anything, to push us over the edge. We find it in our *obstructions*, even the tiny ones. Here's where the little daily things send us over the top. We start a fight with our partner about menial household tasks or pick on our associates about business protocol. We're going to find some order *somewhere*, dammit. We snap at the kids. We glare at anything in our line of sight.

We can avoid the particularly unproductive state of overwhelm by addressing our bevy of concerns before we ever reach the glare-and-snap phase. One could devote a whole book to task management (and many wonderful authors have done just that), so we'll just look at things energetically. We'll shift, prioritize, and set intentions for the results we want.

Try a new kind of prioritizing: look for the feel good. Yes, there are the critical tasks you know are most important and urgent, but there are also usually items on your list that you know will help you *feel better*. Feeling better will help you find the energy and motivation to address *all* the items on your to-do lists—especially the tough ones! So start by just choosing three things that *you feel like doing*. They can be three tiny obstructions that you're sick of thinking about, or the three most pressing concerns on your mind, or a trio mixture from any of the categories. It's up to you. Just choose based on what you *want* to do; choose what *feels* good. And complete the tasks. Start chipping away. As you return to the list for more, acknowledge your progress as you see all your tasks in one place, organized (instead of flitting all around your mind, keeping you awake at night).

If you feel inspired to work on your uncertainties category, start breaking down the items with missing information into workable tasks: people to call, decisions to make, places to look for the information you need. Identify the nature of the missing piece and let it guide you to the next step, so you're no longer looking at a don't-know-what-to-do task; you're looking at a specific place to start.[15]

Maybe you're not finding natural shifts, and prioritizing the feel-good isn't working for you either. If so, we'll have to pull out the big guns of intention. This is for the seriously stuck and freaked out (and for those who already regularly make lists, but are still overwhelmed). It takes time, but if implemented regularly, it can change your life.

In the space next to your to-do tasks in each of the five areas, jot down:

1. a short intended result
2. the feelings that would come with it.

Samples from my list above would break down like this:

ACTIONS: Taxes—*processed/compiled my portion, owed what was expected, easily paid. Psyched!*

EMOTIONAL CONCERNS: Is R mad at me?—*had an easy, honest discussion. Relieved.*

IMPLEMENTATIONS: Get in better shape—*started walking 20 min. each a.m. Feel great.*

OBSTRUCTIONS: Dishes in the sink—*did them, now a habit after dinner. Looks nice.*

UNCERTAINTIES: Call guy about studio space—what's his name? *Remembered who told me about him, called him and booked time for a great rate. Excited.*

Clarifying our intended results and corresponding feelings opens us up to receiving help and ideas from the universe, our Creative Team, and whatever other forms of inspiration we access regularly. It's even fun to make a "Universal To-Do List" to accompany the tasks you're taking on yourself. Use it to list all the

15. The very good book *Getting Things Done* by David Allen (Boston: Penguin, 2002) contains a much fuller exploration of how to break down uncertain items into workable steps.

items with which you'd like a little extra divine attention and ask for help.

If you can't be bothered to write down an intended result for an item, it might be something that you're not really committed to completing. Sometimes we decide by *not deciding*. (You know what I mean, all you deadline-missers.) Move on. Cross off the item or throw it into a take-it-up-later folder. The intended results and feelings that motivate you most will bring your critically important items to the surface.

Finally, do your best to take it easy on yourself. We all take on too much sometimes. Remember that the universe has your best interests at heart, every time.

Remember, too, if you can, that we've all *chosen* the conditions of our lives (even the very challenging ones) for some reason. Each and every overwhelming thing on our lists came with a purpose for us. We've energetically invited it to join the party, so whoo hoo! Where there is strong energy, there is *always* a gift. May it surface sooner rather than later!

Unproductive State of Procrastination

Procrastination lures us from our real creative work under the premise of productivity or pleasure.

Ah, procrastination—that sketchy character who likes to sidle up and settle in for a long visit just when it becomes *critical* that we get down to business. Yeah, we've met.

Procrastination tricks us. It lures us from our real creative work under the premise of productivity or pleasure. When putting off an important project, I've created spectacular displays of procrastination. I've felt compelled to dive into organizational tasks (cleaning out junk drawers, catching up on email, doing housework), sensory treats (eating, drinking, exercising, sex), and happy distractions (social-networking sites, calling a friend to chat). I've been happy as a clam to do anything but the *work*, thank you.

Don't get me wrong—I'm not down on diversions. Diversions can help. As you know from our earlier work with shifting, it's more important to get ourselves in a positive state than it is to force something when we're deep in the low and slow vibes of pressure, frustration, and annoyance with ourselves. But still, we all have moments when we *want* to work, we're *ready* to work, and still, we find ourselves dawdling.

Even while writing this book—about flow and creativity, for goodness sakes!—my writing process fell prey to serious procrastination issues. Just weeks away from an important deadline, a chapter was really giving me problems. I wasn't sure how to start it out, and no matter how many times I wrote a new introductory paragraph and tried to get rolling, it just didn't feel or sound right. I had everything in place: superhot caffeinated beverage (check!); minimal distractions—baby and hubby accounted for (check!); all urgent business matters dealt with for the moment (check!); the perfect spot—a nice quiet place with other people nearby, but not bugging me (check!); and an outlet nearby for my laptop (check—and mate!). Everything I "required" for my optimal writing state was in place. Except the actual *words*.

At first it was no big deal. "I'll just work on something else for a while," I thought. So I moved to different chapters where I'd already gotten a good start.

And yeah.... No. I wasn't finding much inspiration there either.

"Maybe I'll just take a break and do some other things," I figured. So I answered some email messages, read the article that a friend was working on, and got a sandwich.

Tried again. No luck.

I sorted photos on the computer and shopped online for a birthday gift.

And tried again. Still, nothing.

So I called to check on Daisy, read my horoscope, got a fresh pot of tea, updated my website, and edited old texts off my cell phone. It was not shaping up to be a stellar day. "Oh well," I thought. "Just an off day. Tomorrow will be better."

Except it *wasn't*. And nor was the day after that. Every time I tried to start writing, I could only think of other activities that

sounded like a better idea. And here's the kicker: I had arranged ten full days to do almost nothing but write—with no responsibilities except making progress on this particular project—and I wasn't getting *any* writing done. The days were ticking by. "What is wrong with me!?," I wondered. I felt guilty and pressured. I didn't normally have this much open time to work, and I was spending this precious time doing what? Reading stale email and deleting ancient attachments? And with my deadline looming! Not good.

So what did I do? Did I get myself back on track by getting into the feeling states of what I *did want*? Did I apply any other of the tools I know to use?

Hell, no! I panicked! I started doing, doing, doing like a nut. I changed the location and time of day for my work sessions. I furiously cleared my chakras. I emailed all my writer friends for advice. I loaded myself up with nutritional supplements until I was peeing neon orange. (These all were fine, but not really inspired, actions.) Finally, I couldn't take it anymore.

I stopped altogether. I couldn't bear to spend one more minute doing pseudo-productive tasks as I failed to make progress on the most important one. Neither the doing-like-crazy approach nor the *shoulds*, even minor ones, were proving effective at getting my flow back in action. I packed up my laptop and notes and called it a day. (Well, I should have officially called it three days). It was noon, so I enjoyed a leisurely lunch. Got a massage when a lucky last-minute appointment opened up. Called back Rebecca Schweiger, an artist I'd been trying to make time to speak with, and had a great, inspiring conversation with her. I browsed in a bookstore. Went home and played with Daisy. Then took a nap. *A nap!* It felt completely *nervy*.

The next day, I consciously took the day off. I didn't even pretend that I was going to write. I left the laptop packed up and hung out with family instead. I was relaxed and rested. And something *clicked*. I thought about something Rebecca had said in the phone call from the day before, which then reminded me of a train of thought I'd had during the massage. And then I remembered something I'd seen in the bookstore. One thought kept leading to another, when I suddenly realized ideas were coming into focus. I started writing just to "get it down," and it was as if the floodgates opened. Previously unrelated concepts seemed to weave themselves together in new ways, and the words started flowing again. The relief I felt was huge—fantastic—and it lifted my sorry vibe into much healthier territory. The rest of my writing days were full and exciting, and more than made up for the earlier ones.

Maybe we can trick ourselves from time to time and escape the nets of procrastination. We can commit to our butts not leaving the chair for one hour, no matter what we accomplish (or don't). We might tell ourselves that we only need to do *one small thing* and then we're off the hook for the day, and we hope that some momentum develops and winches us out of the rut. Perhaps just showing up day after day, being ready and willing, is the gesture that tells the creative powers-that-be we can be entrusted with an important mission. And maybe our attempts, even if fruitless at the time, help polish our skills for those moments when all else falls away, and nothing—not fear, clutter, hunger, a long to-do list, or anything else—can get in the way of delivering energy into a creative form *right now.*

Maybe we're *always* creating, connecting dots in quiet little mosaics deep in our brains (and creative spirits).

Or, again, maybe the answer lies in believing that the universe holds our best interests at heart. Maybe it's in the faith that honoring our current little desires will lead us to our deepest ones. Maybe we are *always* creating, in ways we don't realize, connecting dots in quiet little mosaics deep in our brains (and creative spirits) and readying ourselves for that one special piece to click into place that will allow all the other pieces to suddenly make sense.

Unproductive State of Fear

In order to create, we learn to dance with fear.

Fear can cloud our process anywhere, anytime. It show up as a fear of success, fear of failure, fear of disrupting the parts of our lives that are working, even as a fear of losing the dreadful familiarity of unsatisfactory jobs, relationships, or anything else. (Oh yeah, those devils we know are tenacious buggers.) Fear can lead us deep into the temptations of procrastination and distraction. And it can stop us in our tracks right as we start getting somewhere.

The creative process comes with a lineage of leaping that we're asked to continue each time the ready whiteness appears. And sometimes the self-care prescription, the faith that pieces are somehow coming together, or a belief in divine timing still won't be enough to convince you that you're not just fooling around because you're scared. You very well might be. That's okay. You're putting yourself on the line (if you're doing it right), and that can be daunting. It's not nearly as daunting, however, as *not doing* it at all.

The creative process comes with a lineage of leaping that we're asked to continue each time the ready whiteness appears.

If fear is interfering with your creativity, it's time to identify the heart of issue. What's the core message? Where in your life would the fear do its damage? Do you have a *specific* anxiety related to the success or failure of your current project?

Success-related fears tend to center on relationships and self-worth. "If I were wonderfully successful, would I still be able to be a good partner or parent?" we wonder. Would my friends think I'm a jerk? Would I have start paying for everything all the time? If I get well known, would someone copy my style and steal my thunder, and leave me without any good ideas? What if I'm a huge success, and then my next project tanks? What would I do then?

Failure-related fears highlight issues of identity, social status, and resources: Who do I think I am? What if I spent all this time and money on this project, and it was a huge waste? What if people think it's terrible (and I'm terrible)? What if my spouse's faith in me was unfounded? What if I can't support myself and my family? What if people are embarrassed by me? Embarrassed for me? What if the naysayers were right all along?

Disaster scenarios provide a dramatic fear landscape for us to play with instead of doing our work.

Disaster scenarios provide a dramatic fear landscape for us to play with instead of doing our work. They highlight absurd, usually unfounded ways that parts of our lives and aspirations would be affected by our work: What if I have to travel all the time on exotic shoots, and my wife has an affair? What if I get crazy famous, and someone kidnaps my dog? What if my show is a huge success, and I have no time to date and can't meet anyone and never have kids? What if I spend too much time in drafty spaces sculpting,

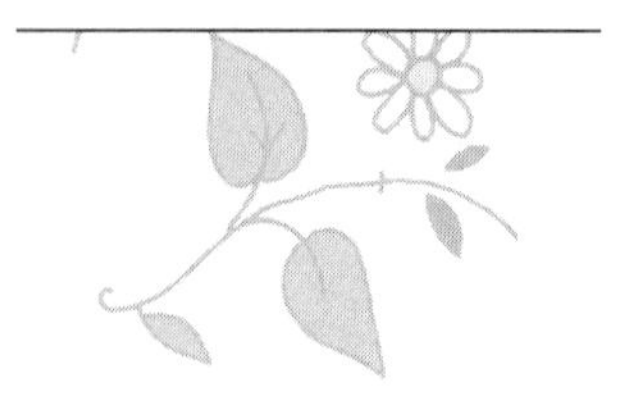

and I get a chronic illness? What if my kids hate me for taking time away from them, and they grow up to be mass murderers? What if I have to eat out all the time and have a heart attack and die?

And there are the lifestyle-based fears: If I'm really good, I might have to work a lot harder, a lot more often. I like my coworkers now—I'd never get to see them. What if I had people taking my picture all the time and had to get dressed up everywhere I went? How exhausting!

Some of these fears probably sound ridiculous, but I guarantee you, *someone* out there has used each of these—or ones more outlandish—as an excuse to resist starting or progressing on a creative work. And deep down, each of us probably has come up with a couple doozies of our own.

So the first thing to do if you're feeling shut down by fear might be to get to the bottom of what your fear is *really* about. Keeping after it until you get to the absurd levels above is one of the most disarming things you can do to a stubborn fear. Start by asking yourself the simple question: "If I ______ (move forward, am hugely successful, finish this piece), what am I afraid might happen?" Follow up your response by asking, "And what would *that* mean?" Ask the latter question several times, until the really interesting stuff starts to emerge. (This is a great exercise to do by taking turns with a friend, by the way).

If your fear remains potent (no absurdity in sight), start shifting into a more powerful place by going over ways that you've met similar challenges in the past and survived, or better yet, thrived. Tell a trusted confidante about one or two of your fears, and ask them for help in seeing the situation another way. Pray, meditate, or intend for peace of mind and confidence to move forward. Ask for signs and models of those people in your situation who have found happiness and fulfillment, or ask directly for innovative solutions to appear.

But most importantly, *put yourself in the feeling state of what you want.* Fears are all about indulging our tendencies to think about what we don't want, remember? I suspect that with the right (well, *wrong*) vibes, you could probably get even the most bizarre disaster scenarios to come true. So get off 'em. Get clear on what you

do want, what the "dream scenario" is. Use your finale thinking. Start feeling how amazing it would be to have people thrillingly responding to you and your work, to have your family thriving, your love relationship rich and energized, your sense of self brimming with purpose and fulfillment.

If you find yourself slipping back into fear, consciously imagine a moment that would represent happy success for you in an area where you typically feel anxiety. Craft a great new scenario to replace your fear-based version. Imagine the sensory qualities of the moment: What do you see, hear, smell? What are you wearing? Are there other people there? What are they doing? Hugging you? Toasting you? Clapping? Smiling? Thanking you? What do you *feel?* (This is extra important.) A quiet sense of gratitude? Contented pleasure? Warm excitement? Find the most positive feeling in the moment and stoke it into a bonfire of gladness. Let this feeling fill your whole self, edging out fears in the process.

It'll bring you around. It'll calm you down. And most importantly, it will create forward movement. All we usually need to free ourselves from inertia and paralysis is that one little nudge. Feel your way, and you'll start feeling better.

Creative Soul Search

If I weren't so overwhelmed, I'd be able to ____________________

____

____

Staying overwhelmed allows me to ____________________

____

____

When I procrastinate, part of me is probably protecting ________

____

____

My procrastination did resolve with great progress that one time when ______

______

If I trusted that *every part* of my creative process is valuable, my habits would ______

______

I can't believe that for all this time, part of me has been afraid that ______

______

I could probably get over my fear of ______ if I tried ______

______

or asked ______
or stopped ______
or believed ______

I'm really thankful for ______

______

I thought my fear was due to ______

______

But I think it might actually be more about ______

______

The part of me that's *not afraid* knows that ______

______

And this would mean ______

______

CHAPTER TWELVE

Kinks

Kinks in our creativity might last a day, a couple sessions, or a whole season. Sometimes they seem to settle in for years. We can sink deeply into them or let them flow right by, stir up all kinds of goofiness or try to quietly let them pass, but they're real. Funky disturbances *do* exist for many of us, whether we're just getting started, smack dab in the middle, or in the editing stages of creating. And they can be very annoying.

Blocks and Dry-Spell Kinks

What's going on when we find ourselves at a loss for ideas or inspiration? What makes it so hard to find the next piece to the continuing puzzle? What causes a project that was happily rolling along to suddenly grind to a halt?

Sometimes *we* are the blank page upon which the universe is writing.

Sometimes our creative valve is wide open, but we're *downloading*, rather than producing.

You already know that indulging in negative emotions and fear and what's not working will create more of the same. If you're currently struggling with a block, I'll assume that you've done the basics already—you've taken inventory of your feelings and shifted your little self into as positive and upbeat a zone as you can muster—and yet you still feel *empty*.

Well, for one thing, maybe you *are*. Sometimes *we* are the blank page upon which the universe is writing. Perhaps those moments of stillness are necessary in order to *take in* the rich information coming through and process it so that it can find its way into form.

Dry spells and blocks often provide needed breaks from the journey—detours that take us to the exact information we need in order to move forward most effectively. If we embrace the notion of partnership with the universe, we can begin to see temporary lapses in creative flow as purposeful pauses meant to *help us*, not deter us.

Maybe the gap is about timing. Though I hesitate to believe the universe *unable* to deliver any desire spontaneously, I do acknowledge the elegant timing of some of my delayed desires. Sometimes it just seems we must wait, for reasons unclear to us, for the timing to improve so that we can make the best possible use of opportunities, skills, and contacts. Maybe we're not quite as ready as we think. Maybe a better situation than we're able to imagine lies right around the corner for us. Or maybe time and experience will reveal ways in which our current desires will prove more distracting than fulfilling in the bigger picture of our lives. It might seem like an out, but I think most of us can think of at least a few examples of how our seemingly unanswered desires, in hindsight, became blessings.

Sometimes I think our creative valve is wide open, but we're *downloading*, rather than producing. An extra step comes into the creative process, and we find ourselves in gathering-and-synthesis mode rather than direct dictation or production. Downloading causes more than a brief pause; it might feel more like a screeching halt as we quietly absorb and assemble elements that will soon become critical to a piece's foundation.

Lastly, creativity is thwarted when the *essence* of our desires differs from the apparent desire. We get awfully cozy with the condition of wanting, which can mess us up as the possibility of having starts to feel more and more imminent.

So let's see what we can do about it all.

Diversion Dynamics

As we've discussed, the characteristics of our energy and vibration levels allow our connection to Source—ah, our good friend Big Creative—to be open and flowing (yay!) or more constricted and obstructed (crap!). When we're vibrating at a wonderfully high, positive level, we're *connected,* baby! The work gushes out of us. We're excited at its merit. We prepare for presentation. On the other hand, when we're trawling amongst the lower, murkier vibes, the work not only slows down in production, but also often seems lacking when it finally does emerge.

Flow can get temporarily diverted to other important areas—like a river briefly rerouted to make a pond—when we're faced with big life events. When milestones or crossroads come up in our path, I think we sense their importance and shift energetically to pay attention and witness the magnitude. We narrow our focus to the situation at hand—the aging parent, the friend's terminal illness, the cross-country move, the career change or new marriage—and experience significant changes in our artistic flow.

When I was pregnant with our first child, I expected to be a flowing powerhouse! I imagined that I'd be writing songs about the nine months of anticipation, creating a richly textured welcome book for our coming pumpkin, painting murals on the nursery wall. I thought I'd plant bulbs all over the yard, start sewing little hats or blankets. I'd do the basic closet-cleanings of nesting, but also *so much more!* You name it, I'd be doing it.

Instead I was shocked to discover that I, in fact, was inspired to do a whole lot of *nothing.* It was all I could do to run a load of laundry. It wasn't a physical thing—after the first three months I had plenty of strength and stamina; I just didn't feel like creating *one darn thing.* I got down on myself. I worried that when the baby

came I would have no time or spare energy and I'd never be able to produce anything interesting ever again. It felt like my window of purpose and potency was slowly closing, and I was wasting these last precious moments on the couch, watching TV and trying to get myself motivated to empty the dishwasher.

Then it got really tricky: my worry started attracting lots of colorful examples of exactly what I did *not* want. I saw only overwhelmed and haggard-looking moms everywhere. Parent friends seemed to constantly complain about how they had no time for themselves and hadn't worked on anything creative in years. I was *not* digging the feeling and general tone of my expectant life.

So I surrendered. It was clear that my worrying wasn't helping, and so I had to trust that it would all, somehow, unfold in a way that was just right. Growing a baby was new to me and certainly was holding my full attention. Besides, I didn't know what else to do. I decided that I wasn't going to agonize anymore about what might happen. We'd made big changes in our life in the past and always found ways to work them out. And hey! I was contributing to the world and our life by being the "blessed vessel," so if that's all I could manage, well, that was going to have to be enough.

Surrendering proved enough of a shift to start improving what I drew into my daily experience. I began noticing happy parents with adorable, charming kids. I found myself in conversations with hip, productive moms who said that their children had actually improved their time-management skills and brought a ton of inspiration into their work.

And when little Daisy finally arrived, in the flurry of new rhythms and sleep deprivation and visitors that babies bring, I didn't have time to think much about my lack of creative productivity. But a few months later, things started picking up. I found myself making up cute, catchy little kids' songs to sing to her. I started posting on my neglected blog again. Ideas for inventions and projects started forming. I found myself jotting down phrases and designs on paper towels and Post-It notes so as not to forget the little bits of (possible) brilliance coming through. I was inspired and energized to finish my artists' intuition cards and start testing them with friends. A producer for a children's animated series contacted me to write the soundtrack for their new show. At one point, I had to put together BOB—the big-orange-binder—in order to keep track of all the exciting projects surfacing!

I asked myself, "Why all this *now?*" The timing felt far from perfect. I was breast-feeding constantly, our house was a disaster, I was tired, and we were *busy*; this baby was taking up *a lot* of time for such a little thing. But it finally hit me: *the flow was back in place.*

While I was pregnant, the creative valve wasn't closed (or closing) as I'd worried. It was merely being diverted to the *creation of a human being*. I was plugged right in to Source, which was *quite* hard at work through me, and I was being a fantastic channel. And once this particular work was done and the waves calmed down, the flow returned to its former path, stronger and more sparkling than ever. If anything, there seemed to be an increase in creative energy coming down the pike.

Perhaps it was the held-back flow letting loose again that caused the fresh surges of inspiration. Or maybe as we honor opportunities to love and grow, our hearts open, and vibrations lift in ways that allow our valve to grow even wider. Whatever the reason, I find it a relief to discover that there does seem to be a natural cycle at work with creativity, and anytime we feel it's not quite *gushing*, we serve our work best by resting assured—trusting, completely calm and confident—that the flow will return.

Fields at Rest

Sometimes our creative pauses are meant as periods of reflection and growth, asking us to take a break for the *sake* of the work, not its detriment. Maybe we're meant to replenish and strengthen ourselves from time to time, and if we don't, it gets done for us.

I grew up in a farm town in Illinois, where the ride to school every day clacked by in long rhythmic rows of corn, soybeans, and alfalfa. For every few meticulously planted fields, there would be

By allowing our personal fields to rest, we show faith that they will yield for us again.

one sitting unplanted, overgrown and neglected looking. I asked my dad one day why the farmers didn't plant *all* the fields and get the most crops they could. He told me that in order to get the best yield from the land, growers had figured out that it's better to let the fields rest for a season every couple years. This rest period allows the soil to recover and soak up more nutrients, and to be more fertile for the next planting.

I think the same thing happens to us, whether we consciously choose this process of not. We experience periods of wonderful productivity, bumper crops of beautiful works, and the abundance fuels us. "I can do more!" we think. "This is amazing!" We float on the high of the harvest. We can go on for several seasons this way. The thrill of the yield is one of the unmatchable gifts in a creator's life. But somewhere along the line, we might notice that there are diminishing returns in our fields. And it's exactly at this point that we are wise to let them rest.

Maybe this is when the flow seems to cease for a bit, or when we find ourselves more tired or distracted than usual. Maybe it's when we get sick—our bodies, minds, and spirits colluding to slow us down, to allow for maintenance repairs and nourishing connections to take place in our cells, neural pathways, and energy.

In any case, if we occasionally sense a need to step back (or step away altogether), honoring that urge might allow all the disparate bits of inspiration that contribute to a whole piece to come together. By allowing our personal fields to rest, we show faith that they will yield for us again, in perhaps more bountiful ways than in past seasons.

So *be not afraid,* dear artist. Whether it's just one sublime seed incubating or a whole field that's taking a well-earned rest, the blooms will come again.

The Blessed Pause

In music and poetry, the *caesura* is a device used to indicate a pause—a brief cessation in the verse or music. Caesuras offer a small, meaningful break in the line, a way to offset a phrase for more emphasis and significance.

When I find myself in a sudden stop after a fairly steady run of inspiration, I frequently wonder if it isn't a subtle caesura, sent by Source to ask me to take note of something important. Am I at a critical jumping-off point for a new thought? Did I just get down something that needs a bit more exploration or consideration before I leave it? Is there something coming up that I need to prepare to hear just a little bit more carefully? These moments drop into my consciousness like a *command to stare*. I feel a total compulsion to space out and, well, look and listen.

I used to fight these caesuras, thinking they were just one more way my busy brain was trying to get out of finishing the task at hand, but I've come to be more gentle with myself about them, just in case they're actually inspiration trying to penetrate. Remember the great scene in the library in the Wim Wenders movie *Wings of Desire?* It showed angels, leaning in close to those studying and writing, whispering inspiration softly into the ears of those in their care. Now when I feel these little urges to stop and gaze for a moment, I imagine that it might be my spiritual creative team, offering help. I open to the possibility that I might be getting something, a hint of one of these special whispers.

If we can deeply embrace the idea that the universe always presents us with the perfect opportunities, at the perfect times (a concept I know can be challenging at times), it's possible to see disruptions in our inspiration as blessings, rather than inconveniences.

Think back to a career opportunity you believed you were ready for, far before you could have taken best advantage of it. Or the client you desperately wanted, but later heard was a total nightmare. Maybe you can recall seeing a car accident and realizing that if you hadn't done that brief errand, you might have been the victim. Even when the events don't turn out the way we might prefer in a given moment, I believe that trusting that our lives are, *as a whole,* unfolding in a positive, purposeful way allows for a more energetic, confident outlook than the alternative, victim mentality.

So as the caesuras appear in our days or creative processes, it may serve us best to see them as blessed pauses. Perhaps this is the break that will allow you to remember that great paint or gemstone

or fabric you had stashed away somewhere, or the metaphor that will really make this piece come alive. Perhaps this (interruptive) phone call will spark a new way of looking at your current work. Maybe being late to this appointment will put you exactly where you *need* to be today, instead of where you were scheduled to be. It's a game of trust, and if we want to stay focused on the most positive, most exciting aspects of our lives, we play.

Editing Kinks

Lord, do we fear amputation.

It's easy to get attached to our work, even the less-than-stellar examples. Our pieces become familiar, dear to us. They feel more like our limbs than chapters or photographs or colors on a board. We know it's not particularly healthy, but still we cling to them, shelter them. We can't help it.

But I Love That Piece!

Editing must take place for the greater good of the work. And this daunting understanding can hold us hostage.

Editing requires faith in our ability to know immediately if a choice works or not. Our uncertainty results in hard drives, attics, and file cabinets overloaded with the creative attempts we refuse to delete or destroy. *We might need it someday.*

We stay stubbornly attached to a preconceived outcome, even as we sense a piece moving in a new direction. It's terribly distressing when we've put in quality work, made real progress on a piece, to discover that in order to move forward, something we love needs to be released, edited, or cut. But, indeed, for the sake of the work, we've got to "kill [our] darlings," as writer Kate Mansfield advised.

The moment something becomes too precious in our art, we become beholden to it. It distracts from the greater piece. It's an awful feeling, having to basically self-destruct and rebuild, even if it's just a tiny aspect of ourselves, but editing must take place for the greater good of the work. And this daunting understanding—at a deep, maybe subconscious, level—can hold us hostage until we are ready to bring the paring knives to the project.

But It's So Close!

Perhaps you're not attached to a particular outcome as much as obsessed with a piece's *unmet potential.* It's possible to rework something to death, to be so committed to its promise that you revise and edit and overdo it until you've completely butchered the thing. I've done this myself and have nicknamed the process "reworking syndrome."

Reworking syndrome often appears in student art, where emerging artists have vision and dedication, but not the skills to pull off an ambitious project. The paper wears thin where repeated erasures (or other kinds of editing) took place, as the artist was trying to get it just right. Ghosts clearly remain of former attempts. It's unnerving. Audiences become uneasy when experiencing art that tries this hard (and knows its shortcomings so well). We do better when we fail harder, when we're bold with our imperfect strokes. Viewers engage more confidently with work that is daring, even if it is faulty.

Viewers engage more confidently with work that is daring, even if it is faulty.

Reworking syndrome pops up frequently at workshops or conferences where up-and-coming artists gather. After reworking a song or short story a half dozen times upon the advice of a seasoned professional, rising artists can't understand why it's still not working. "But I *did* what she suggested I do!" they insist. "I changed that line! I edited the ending!"

Songwriter Jeffrey Steele referred to this overblown commitment to a piece while giving a master class on writing. He lamented the fact that so many writers would play a song at a conference one year and then come back the following year and play the *same song*, with just a few small changes here and there. He shook his head in amazement at the absurdity of this one-tracked path. For someone like him, an outrageously prolific writer, it made no sense that someone would hack away at a single song for over a year.

"Listen to me, people," he said very seriously. Then slowly and deliberately, he shouted, "Write a new fucking song!"

His words reverberated through the crowd, and not just because of the strong language. We've all had pieces that feel *so close*—just a twinkle away from something really important—but don't

realize their potential. Maybe the works are fine, and it's the timing or market that's not right. Maybe it's meant to be one rung on the ladder that leads to our unique style and grace. Maybe we're not ready for what might come our way were it to really land for us. Or maybe *it's just not there yet,* and a thousand songs from now, you'll see exactly where you were in your development and how far you've come. But you've got to write those thousand songs to get there.

Living on the leading edge of creativity can be very uncomfortable.

Release that tight hold on your babies. Present them to whomever you want, take the feedback for what it is, and move on. Or put your precious potentials in a box and move on. Or make a beautiful diorama to them and move on. Or say a prayer of thanks for each step on the path, and move on.

But do move on. You've got new fucking songs to write.

Summit-Sickness Kinks

Kick-ass creativity leads to thrilling opportunities, but it's your talent and commitment that does the rest.

Living on the leading edge—the kick-ass edge—of creativity can be very uncomfortable at times. The spectacularly rich stimulation of finally meeting our desires can feel like just too much to process. It often sends us on weird little trips as we sort it all out.

As you find yourself in sight of your deepest desires (or actually experiencing them!), your clear, strong energy can help you avoid common pitfalls and just enjoy the present.

Oxygen Glut

After living at a high altitude for many years, Mark and I have noticed that when we visit our families in the Midwest, our bodies don't seem to know what to do with all that lowland oxygen. Instead of feeling pumped up and energized to go run a marathon (since distance runners train at altitude, right?), we typically find ourselves sleepy and lethargic.

We're in *oxygen glut*. Having too much of a nourishing thing can leave us just as off-center as not having enough.

Meeting a long-held desire can create a similarly sludgy quality in our energy. While working toward a clear finish line, we have consistent motivation. We are able to chart our progress and feel ourselves draw closer to our goal with each concerted effort. Our long-term familiarity with this striving, productive identity can contrast strongly with the relative stillness of the newer, "Wow, I finally made it" self. From this uneasy place, successful artists sometimes end up romanticizing the former, more comfortable and familiar state of working toward the goal. They then conclude that their hard-won desires aren't creating those hoped-for feelings after all, which gives birth to a cynical, "It's not all it's cracked up to be" identity.

Desires can indeed reveal unexpected characteristics once we hold them in our hands. As we grow accustomed to their weights or textures, we sometimes get uncomfortable. "It feels weird. I'm not sure about it," we think. Before we've even absorbed our big moment, opportunities for negative focus arise and start poking at us!

A desire might not be everything you expected, but it's certainty got *some* benefits, right? Surely there are gifts you didn't even *imagine*. Consciously use your focus. See the positives. Be thankful. And in no time, you'll shake off the funk of being ridiculously successful. (Do be quick about it if you'd like to have any friends left when you emerge.)

Savor the Summit

When you reach a milestone, give yourself the gift of acknowledgment. Enjoy the view from the top of the mountain you've just climbed, even if it allows you to see new, greater peaks in the distance.

Resist the temptation to rush right past the sweet spot of a met desire and into the throes of the next project. Yes, I know, there are new opportunities to explore, possibilities brewing as we speak! Stop anyway. *Stop.* Smile. Breathe for a moment. Take it in.

Mark the occasion with a gesture that recognizes your accomplishment.

Take a walk in nature, and on your walk, talk—and listen—to yourself. Imagine that you're speaking for your spiritual creative team as they shower you with pride and warm wishes. Give yourself the feedback you crave (perhaps secretly), whether it be acknowledgement of your hard work, astonishment at your triumph, thrilling wonder at what lies ahead, or remembrances of the journey that lead you to now.

Buy yourself a gift, preferably of the delightfully sensory persuasion—beautiful meals, massages, and shiny things are always fun.

Or sit down and write yourself a letter. Write to your future self, about how you feel today, what this project means to you, how excited you are, or even how daunted or tentative you might feel. Or write lovingly to your past self, encouraging that person to carry on, as good things await!

Just find *some way* that helps you absorb the full spectrum of the moment, and to energetically chronicle it for yourself. It's far too easy to find life whooshing us right past the parts where we should be marking a step of the journey.

Serve your energy and honor your work by pausing to acknowledge what you've accomplished. Complete the circuit.

Creative Soul Search

When a block or dry spell affects my work, my usual reaction is to

____

____

The next time it happens, I'm going to try ____________________

____

____

If my creative energy feels diverted right now, it's understandable, since it's probably going toward ______________________________

____

____

While my ______________________________ (areas of my life) feel productive and rich, it's comforting to think the quiet of my ______________________ might be just a "field at rest."

I've been saving ______________________________ (previous versions of a piece) for an awfully long time without looking at it or thinking about it.

I've probably reached the end of my work on ______________, and should move on, as much as I love it.

If I were really a kick-ass creator, I'd produce ______________ (number of works) ______________________ (this often).

I could probably accomplish this if I tried ______________________

____

____

or asked ______________________________

or stopped ______________________________

or believed ______________________________

I'm really thankful for ______________________________

____

____

When I ______________________ (accomplishment), I'm going to mark the occasion by ______________________________

____

____

The greatest compliment someone could give me or my work is

____

____

CHAPTER THIRTEEN

Action Paths

Action, energy, and intention—they're three happy peas in a pod. This happy trio works so beautifully together that they rarely find themselves apart. In this section, we'll explore how specific paths of action can be applied to various aspects of the modern artist's experience. We'll look at how to expand our industry presence, fine-tune our readiness for the biggest of big gigs, and script with style for really cool results.

Action Path: Your Big Gig

If you've been applying the energy tools, you're probably picking up some nice momentum right about now. You're getting into the idea and practice of consistently nudging your energy and conscious thoughts in the exact direction of your dreams. You've learned how

How would you make sure your big gig really got you noticed for a more lasting impact?

to deal with the dissenting and distracting voices around you (or inside you), and you're hopefully already finding focus useful and effective in little everyday things as well as the big artistic visions of our lives. So what's next?

You tell me. I want you to imagine that the most thrilling opportunity you've ever imagined for yourself—I like to think of it as "the big gig"—has just dropped into your life. And it's *tomorrow.*

Really get into the flow of this. Make it real for you. Imagine you've just made arrangements with your honey, the office, kids, and the dog, and you're starting to pack and prepare your materials. This is the moment you've waited for most of your creative life. You're finally getting your *shot.*

Take a moment to imagine people discovering your work—hearing your song for the first time, seeing you captivatingly take the lead role in the Broadway play, casting their eyes upon your paintings or sculptures at the fabulous Chelsea gallery opening. For that matter, imagine that *it goes great.* You are a hit! The buzz on the street is all about where have you *been* all this time!? You are poised for the fame, fortune, and opportunities that you've always hoped for.

Can it really happen? Of course it can.

Do you have everything in place in order to allow it to happen most easily, quickly, and stresslessly? How would you make sure your big gig really got you noticed for a more lasting impact? Are you ready to *take* the opportunity and really make it shine?

Hmm, let's see. There are always practical issues to consider.

First of all, *would people be able to find you?* Do you have a website? Do you have business materials like cards, letterhead, and a professional, working email address? Have you got a potential manager or agent (or a devoted, organized friend to act like one) who could step in to help handle opportunities as they start to flow?

Are you ready to serve your adoring public? Is your information organized and compelling? Are your products in stock? Is there a way for people to sign up for a mailing list to keep up with your brilliant future releases?

Will people be excited when they find you? Is your image well developed for what you wish to accomplish? Are you healthy and comfortable with your appearance? Do you have ways to stay calm, collected, confident, and energetic when in the spotlight or while maintaining a jam-packed schedule?

Really?

This is the moment where most of us realize (with a rapidly increasing heart rate) that there are about eighteen significant things we really should do in order to optimize this opportunity for best effect.

It's the *reverberations* that might follow a pinnacle experience that also deeply motivate us.

We probably have the basic elements ready to go: the works are ready, we know the piece, we can patch something together to serve as a bio and dig up a photo for the program. But are we ready to seize the deeper fullness of the moment? Are we ready to absorb what we really imagine is the *heart* of this experience? After it's over, will we be able to see that it acted as a springboard to great feelings and more thrilling opportunities, rather than an end in itself?

In our art, fantasized opportunities tend to have a goal within the goal—a desire for the *core essence* of the experience that reaches far beyond the surface benefits. We're really after the *feelings*, remember? It's not that we want merely exposure—perhaps it's that we crave *admiration*. We seek not only the financial reward of high-priced sales of our works, but we also seek the *validation* that they are recognized as that valuable, or the *freedom* to work in ideal materials and time frames.

Looking at our big gigs in this way, it becomes easier to see that it's not only the experience of the big gig that we desire. It's the *reverberations* that might follow a pinnacle experience that also deeply motivate us. It's here we imagine that we'll most clearly experience the approval, freedom, security, resources—whatever we really deeply desire. It's in the *aftermath* of a pinnacle experience that the response stage of the creative cycle takes place, and that stage, like it or not, offers us direct feedback on the work and how we fit into the larger picture of our field.

Why not create at least the best *groundwork* for thrilling reverberations? We work so hard to prepare our creative work for presentation, yet often neglect other areas of our lives that directly impact critical and commercial success.

So as we energetically disarm the niggling fears that crouch around in the shadows of our big dreams, it's important to also examine the nuts and bolts of our preparation. If we don't think we're (at least mostly) ready, we'll worry that we aren't. This worry can absolutely grow as powerful as other limiting beliefs that we're not good enough, young enough, attractive enough or anything *else* enough. (And we definitely don't need to be dealing with any more energy landmines than is necessary.)

My formerly vague list of "things I really should do" came into crystal clear focus when I had a fantastic opportunity come my way one spring

After a significant amount of back-and-forth delays with a producer, I got an email notifying me that I was being considered to perform on a huge, nationally syndicated TV talk show in a matter of days. After the first rush of elation (and rush to my husband's office to share the good news!), I slowly floated back to earth and started thinking of all the things I should really get done in case it all came together at the end of the week.

Here are the first ten tasks on the list that I made (while on the treadmill, mind you—sure, *now* I wasn't going to waste a single second):

1. Get my website updated! Redesign it!? Find a good mailing list program
2. Get a more stylish haircut, teeth whitened?, and lose fourteen pounds in next four days
3. Practice song until I don't have to worry I'll screw up
4. Get some ideas for agents to contact in case opportunities come up afterwards

5. Check to make sure song is up on iTunes and that CDs are stocked in stores
6. Think about who I can invite to taping without hurting major feelings or making myself too nuts or nervous
7. Get new business cards with the right cell number on them (!)
8. Check performing-rights society to make sure it's registered properly for royalty stuff
9. Write up page on site for "More Perfect World Foundation" to accept donations
10. Look up some breathing or centering exercises to do before playing to keep from wigging out

After listing a dozen more really important things that I needed to do before making my national TV debut, I realized that I was energetically contributing to the delays and uncertainty in the situation. My really-should-do list was screwing things up! On the surface, I convinced myself that all the pieces would fall into place if I got to go perform, but deep down I was freaking out.

"What if I look frumpy?" I worried. (I was still getting off the last of my baby weight. Oh yeah, and the ten extra pounds I carried around before the baby.) What if industry people flood to my site, and it looks completely unprofessional and outdated, and they dismiss me? What if tons of people want to sign up on a mailing list, and there isn't one to sign up on? What if I really nail it—play perfectly, like in my most wonderful dreams—and I have nothing in place to support it, so nothing happens?

The opportunity dissipated; the show decided against the music segment. I was disappointed, but a part of me was relieved. Once again I had a beautiful expanse of time in which to get going on those really-should-do tasks. And so I did.

With my newly invigorated intention, things started really flowing. I found a great, affordable website designer and mailing-list program. I ordered snappy new business cards. I stepped up

my exercise program and image maintenance. I began rehearsing with intention and excitement, using images of the show's stage as my own little mental buzz factory. All the things that I thought I could do *someday* moved to the top of the *now* list, suddenly feeling fun and exciting to check off. I began feeling lighter and more energized with each step I completed.

The following fall, I got a call that a new, different opportunity had come up for me. And I was ready and willing, 100 percent. That opportunity lead to my song "This Is Our Life" making a fantastic national impact that changed my life (and lives of many listeners who thoughtfully wrote to me) in amazing, wonderful ways. And I firmly believe it would not have happened had the chance come when I had a list full of really-should-do tasks.

Maybe you're confused and thinking: "Hey! But I thought we were supposed to do what *feels good!* I thought doing stuff we think we *should do* is a big draining distraction!?"

I hear you. It's hard to see the distinction sometimes. I'm talking about the really irritating energy leaks, here—the stuff that makes you worry, makes you feel bad and deflated every time you think about it not being done. This isn't deciding to get the dishwasher unloaded instead of taking a nap—this is bigger picture stuff.

Let's kick the *should* out it. Perhaps we can think of tasks that contribute to a healthy, working body, mind, creative flow, and business as foundation tasks. These are the tasks we complete in order to answer preparation-oriented questions, like "Am I skilled enough?" or "Am I ready?" If you sense that an undertaking would *bring you into better alignment with the creative future you want,* it's a foundation task.

Keeping this foundation task list clear and done is a nuts-and-bolts way to be vigilant in your everyday business part of your journey. If it helps, think of each task you complete as freeing you from the little anchors that pin you down and keep you from moving up into the realm you desire. "Yep that's right. There goes another one." And you're floating up a bit higher, a bit freer already. Very good.

Banishing Drains

As fun and helpful as it is to collect and direct fresh new energy, it's just as important to find and close off places where your current energy is draining away. Scan the areas of your life that are negatively dominating your attention (and probably draining your energy).

Jump-start some new energy into your life by noticing your *tolerations.* If something (or someone) bugs you, drains you, or frustrates you on a regular basis, you've probably got a toleration. When we're surrounded with a multitude of these annoyances and obstacles, our energy gets diverted from more fulfilling paths and instead directed toward "finding one pen in this house that works, dammit!" or wondering, "Why, why, do we answer her calls when we know we're going to just get dumped on!?"

What are you tolerating that pulls your energy away from the activities and people that stimulate and fulfill you?

Make your spaces *work for you.* If they're not making you feel *good,* they're not working.

What are you tolerating that pulls your energy down and away from the activities and people that stimulate and fulfill you? Make a list. Which of these could you address and eliminate with a little dedicated time and effort? Is there a specific area of your life where you notice a preponderance of tolerations?

Environment can be a biggie. It doesn't matter a whit how it actually looks, by the way—what matters is how you *feel* about your spaces. Does your messy house weigh you down and depress you the minute you walk in? Are there a lot low-energy elements like dirt, uninvited critters, clutter, or garbage surrounding you? Do you feel more *alive* with your things strewn around you? Do you love the stimulating chaos of a studio that's jam-packed with projects? Do you feel happily ensconced and potent when surrounded by a dozen works in progress and feel resentful when you're forced to tidy up at the end of each session? Or does this kind of atmosphere leave you feeling paralyzed and stuck in the middle of a dozen things?

Make your spaces *work for you.* If they're not making you feel *good,* they're not working. Make a snappy task journal to get you going, if you like. Make collages or write out descriptions of how you'd like to feel in the spaces you regularly inhabit. Let your visions help you customize each room. Choose to see your surroundings as a creative project. Work toward creating the kind

Try making an "environmental life portrait" by looking to your spaces for clues to what's working and what may be clogged or in need of nurturing.

of environment that you want (inspiring, functional, energizing spaces) instead of what you don't (anything that makes you feel uncomfortable, tired, or bad about yourself). You might even try making an "environmental life portrait" by looking to your spaces for clues to what's working and what may be clogged or in need of nurturing in your life. What rooms are full of old junk? Which are bare or neglected? Draw your own correlations between areas in your home and parts of your life they might represent.

How are your relationships? Again, let go of any "objective" analysis. *You* know if there are problems to address, no matter how perfect a relationship might look from the outside. If changes need to be made, and you (or your partner, best friend, kids, parents) are resisting them, it's likely that your emotional energy is heading here more than toward your creative flow. Work on the issues through your creative form, if you aren't doing that already. Talk about them. Decide what result you want, and script those results however you like. Take inspired action when it arises.

And speaking of people-based issues, are there any energy vampires in your life? Call them what you wish—crazymakers, toxic people, drama queens—but most of us know a few people who really drain us. They corner us with their dramas, ignore our thoughtful feedback, and move on when they sense our interest (or sympathy) fading. If you're finding someone leeching off your energy in this way, it's time to lay down the law with some creative passive aggression (or just plain aggression!). Take a break from the relationship. Stop picking up the phone, engaging via email, or agreeing to get together for a while. It might be hard, but do it. I know you. You are one brilliant, helpful, insightful person. And I also know that you can get sucked into someone else's problem vortex at the drop of a hat. It's time to break free, even if taking part of these dramas occasionally makes you feel wise or needed. You've got your own fish to fry, my little amateur therapist. Tend to your own fire.

How about money? Are you up to your eyeballs in debt? Money stress pulls at the same reptilian parts of our brains that manage survival. The autonomic nervous system responds to overdue bills and mounting debt as if our food, air, or safety is being threatened.

I don't know how you'll prefer to address it—perhaps a lucrative side job, more industrious marketing of your skills, or even getting a loan, grant, gift, or patron will be possibilities for you. But if money is frequently on your mind, your creative current is being diverted from its happiest path. (Conversely, if you're scraping by, but really aren't bothered by it, you're fine. Carry on.)

Action Path: Interchange

Presenting our work for witness lets us grow, improve, and better understand the resonant nature of what we do. The work must not languish in the obscurity of our laptops or studios. You know it's true: it's got to get *out there* in order to get the results you desire.

Creators crave opportunities for presentation, impact, and interchange.

Expose Yourself to Your Neighbors

In quantum physics, the Copenhagen Interpretation established that particles act differently when under observation. They, in fact, become a *form*, choosing to shift from a state of endless potential into something of fixed character, when the observation takes place.[16] Perhaps our art is like this too. It needs to be presented for observation in order to be cemented into being.

In any case, creators certainly crave opportunities for presentation, impact, and interchange. Maybe we shouldn't care what anyone else thinks, but we do. Finding and nurturing a creative community (and its associated spectrum of response) helps fill the gaps in the often isolated life of the modern artist. Peers can reassure us when we're panicked, support us when we falter, and share in our excitement when we make progress.

Do you know your local peers? Have you asked for help from more accomplished artists in your area? Have you been open to mentoring emerging local creators? Yes, you'll find some characters. (Guess what? You'll find even weirder weirdos on the national

16. McTaggart, Lynne. *The Intention Experiment: Use Your Thoughts to Change the World.* New York: Harper Element, 2008.

level.) You'll also probably discover some very cool new people who may be tapped into to local happenings that you've missed.

Do you know the rhythms of regional opportunities for exposure, such as yearly exhibits, deadlines, and competitions? Do you attend events in your area, even if you're not personally involved?

It's vibrationally satisfying to find *your people*.

Even if your local creative community isn't the hottest scene on the planet (and *no one* thinks theirs is, by the way), make a concerted effort to support it. Go to the opening, the late-night performance-art piece, or the film showcase. Offer to sell CDs at a friend's gig. Wander around and chat with artisans at the craft market. Play pro bono at the fundraising event. Your efforts will create excellent vibe (and karma) around your own fledgling pursuits down the road. You also might discover some promising possibilities for collaboration or synergy with other artists once you better know their skill sets.

Another great thing about local events is that they're rarely intimidating. Your community can be a great testing ground for trying new things and stretching your boundaries in a nonthreatening environment.

If you feel inspired to take a leadership role or to volunteer to help out at local events, you may find yourself with unique opportunities to meet industry professionals you respect and admire. One summer, I volunteered with a local concert booker to transport artists from the airport to their lodging in town (about a one-hour drive each way). Sure, it was a time commitment, but I got to share relaxed, interesting conversations with Grammy winners, folk icons, and personal musical heroes of mine. Other cool opportunities might be found by volunteering to attend to a green room, book speakers or panelists for a gathering, or promote an upcoming event to regional media.

Expose Yourself to the General Public

Attending larger industry events provides a great opportunity to network, make friends in other regions, hone your craft, and showcase your work to a larger audience. Beyond the career-enhancing potential of these gatherings, it's vibrationally satisfying to find *your people.* When sharing a spirit of belonging, mutual respect, and open resources, a group of like-minded creators can be one of an artist's strongest assets.

But let's be honest—it can be challenging too. Conferences or workshops can tip you a tad off balance. You're choosing to surround yourself with other creators, and some of them might be really good! You might feel less unique, less special than you'd like. It'll be almost impossible to keep from evaluating your place on the artistic totem pole (even with all the ego pitfalls brought on by that hellish exercise).

Be mindful of your energy as you engage with other participants, as there can occasionally be serious posturing at these gatherings. (I don't mean *you*, of course. You *never* posture!)

There are specific ways to maximize your time and opportunities at an industry event or weekend. Here are some ideas for presenting yourself and your work in the best light possible. I've included the underlying energetic messages you'll send out (and thus affirm for yourself) with each action.

Beforehand. Pay attention to opportunities for showcasing your work. You'll probably be required to send materials in advance (with your registration and a small fee). Do it. *It's worth it.* If nothing else, the showcase deadline will help you get a strong piece finished. If you're chosen to showcase, your work will speak for you, allowing your peers to find you and industry people to notice you on their own terms. It will also demonstrate that you have your act together, which is always reassuring to higher-ups. Another approach is to send an advance email or note to an industry professional you hope to meet at the conference. Something short and charming that mentions your appreciation of their work should do the trick.[17] It'll get your name on their radar and also give you a conversation starter if you see him or her lingering alone somewhere between sessions. *Vibe: Presentation is a natural part of the creative process. I welcome feedback and opportunities.*

17. See Carolyn See's terrific book, *Making a Literary Life,* for more in-depth guidance on writing charming notes and forging industry contacts in your field.

Be bold and venture out there solo.

Go alone, if possible. Be bold and venture out there solo, and you'll talk with more new people and be more available for chance opportunities. You'll also get to refresh your sense of personal identity and be able to speak about your work without the need to frame it in a certain way for an already-familiar friend or partner. *Vibe: "My people" are here to be found. I'm up for connecting. I choose my story each time I tell it.*

Be generous with your praise. An authentic, kind word offered at a vulnerable moment can save someone's sanity (and pave the way for some nice camaraderie, or even long-term friendship). *Vibe: Appreciating someone else's skills and talent doesn't diminish mine. I am secure enough to look outside myself and see brilliance in others.*

Be generous with your resources. Help your fellow artists if you can. By sharing what you have (and who you know), you show faith that there are plenty of opportunities for everyone, resulting in a vibration of abundance that can only boomerang back in a lovely way toward you. Your generosity (and apparent security) will also shock the hell out of everybody. *Vibe: There's enough of everything to go around, so there's no need to constrict or hoard. When I share my resources, I realize how many I have.*

Don't be an ass. During sessions, keep your comments to your neighbor short and sweet. Text your buddy later. Offer the same attention to those in the spotlight that you'd appreciate yourself. The most accomplished artists that I've met have also been incredibly gracious people. I guarantee you, Robert Redford and Tom Hanks would not snicker their way through someone's story, song, or explanation of a piece. Hold the persona of the great artist you want to be. *Vibe: Everyone deserves respect and attention when they present a work, including me. There's a gracious, accomplished artist inside of me already guiding my actions.*

Take time to recharge. I've never needed a walk, nap, or meditation as badly as I do during conferences. Maybe it's the full schedule, the contemplation, the note-taking, the chatting with new people, or even the competition that creeps up on me, but I find it critical to recenter and freshen up energetically once or twice a day. *Vibe: There's no need to force things. It's good to rest and rejuvenate. The right opportunities and contacts present themselves in perfect timing.*

Don't eat alone unless you're recharging. Firstly, this looks bad in a place full of people wanting to connect with each other, and secondly, it's wasting valuable opportunities to bond and grow. If you're shy, ask one interesting person from a session if they'd like to join you for lunch and find out as much about them as you can. Be really interested in them and their work. Learn from them. Really listen. If you're outgoing, ask to tag along with an interesting-looking group. Everyone's there to meet people, so usually there's a nice undertone of "the more, the merrier." Do try to be conscious of the us-versus-them (industry/attendee) element of conferences, however. If you spot an all-industry professional group, they may be old friends who rarely have the chance to catch up. Respect their situation and look for some of your peers instead. *Vibe: We're all here to connect. I'm willing to put myself out on a limb because you seem interesting. You are interesting! Resources and wisdom can be found everywhere.*

Concentrate on your peers in general. You're on a path together, one that can inspire *all* of you to great things and exciting contributions. It's human nature to want to "friend *up*"—to become chummy with the biggest wigs you can—but this is tricky business. Everybody knows what's happening when one party wants something from the other; it's not an authentic partnership. With your peers, you can forge real friendships based on mutual admiration and a shared journey. (Anyway, it's a better use of your time. You know those bigwigs that everybody's kissing up to? They've got their *own* friends from back-in-the-day whom they'd like to help.) *Vibe: I respect the potential of my peers and am worthy of their respect. Progress is faster and more fun when we freely exchange support.*

Take feedback for what it is. Some workshops hold critique sessions where budding artist participants can bounce their work off of experienced pros and get some feedback. The common unspoken goal for participants in these sessions is for the professional

The only person who wakes up in the morning and wants to make you a star is *you*.

Pass on anything that leaves you feeling anxious, underqualified, or insecure.

to immediately spot the brilliance in your work and insist you *sign to his company* (best scenario) or *meet her support person*, such as an agent, manager, or publisher (next best scenario). What usually happens, however, is that the professionals politely, maybe even uncomfortably, indicate where a piece could be stronger, more streamlined, or more marketable. Then they move on to the next critique, leaving the budding artist shell-shocked and deflated.

Having sat on both sides of the table (as a hopeful young artist with my song in hand and as a seasoned professional with, hopefully, some wisdom to share), I can offer two insights: (1) opinions of perfection are completely subjective, and (2) the only person who wakes up in the morning and wants to make you a star is *you.* If someone's feedback on your piece resonates with you, great—use it. If it doesn't, try again with someone else, or just trust that you know your work best and move on. Understand that *everyone* else has his or her own self-interest at heart in some way, and if your project doesn't support those self-interests for a given industry professional, you probably won't be starting a relationship. Take help where it's offered, follow up on inspiration, and apply good advice where you recognize it. Try *very hard* to acknowledge to yourself just how subjective the critique process is, no matter how stellar or disappointing the responses to your work may be. *Vibe: I'm secure enough to be open to response, but not dependent on it.*

Protect yourself. If you notice that certain people or activities are pulling your energy down, *opt out.* There's no rule that says you have to attend every single thing. Find the offerings that inspire you and leave you excited to get back to the work. Pass on anything that leaves you feeling anxious, underqualified, or insecure. You can always try it another time. *Vibe: I trust my emotional feedback. When I feel good, I'm literally making more progress than by feeling terrible doing something I "should" do.*

Attend unofficial gatherings and social get-togethers when possible. Visit the bar or social hour in the evenings, even if you're just drinking water. It's the place where you're most likely to find the good gossip, bonding, and a blurred line between the industry and attendee folk. *Vibe: I'm cool, I'm fun, I'm casual. I'd be fun to work with!*

Now go have fun and find your people.

Creative Soul Search

If my big gig dropped into my lap tomorrow and were going to take place in three days, my first response would be ______________________

My secondary response would be ______________________

Something I know I've needed to do for a long time is ______________________

I'm going to start working on this on ____________ (time and day) by ______________________

When I'm with my creative peers, I generally find myself feeling ______________________

A person who exemplifies kick-ass creativity for me is ______________________

What is this person doing that I am not currently doing? ______________________

I usually find that my creative community feels ________________

____

____

I'm inspired to improve or participate in my local creative community by ________________

____

____

I'd love to go to a big conference in order to ________________

____

____

I could probably work it out to go if I tried ________________

____

____

or asked ________________________________
or stopped ________________________________
or believed ________________________________

I'm really thankful for ________________________

____

____

CHAPTER FOURTEEN

Kick-Ass Specifics: Q & A

Information is empowering. Clear, defined steps are motivating. When we have sites to explore, resources to consult, and people or companies to contact, we feel more empowered to act boldly in industries known for their exclusivity and gatekeepers.

In this dialogue, I've included specific resources—wherever possible—for getting started or making progress in various genres. The following questions represent issues that have come up over and over again with my creative clients. My hope is that with amplified energy, full knowledge of what you want, and a few concrete contacts and ideas, you'll be ever more likely to honor Big Creative when it calls.

Leap! Begin stepping out in new, exciting ways!

The world is waiting on *you.*

Start small and manageable, and be brave.

Q: "I think I'm ready to begin selling my work, but I don't know where to start."

A: Good for you! Start small and manageable, and be brave. You've been inspired to do these pieces for a reason and you can get them out there. It's never been easier to make your art available to people all over the world.

First, ask yourself some basic questions and do a little homework. Combine your resources with your desires; mix together an evaluation of what you've *got* with the ideas of what you *want.* Some personal reflection and targeted Web searches will likely provide the most efficient and up-to-date information you need. If you're not an experienced Web searcher, ask a computer-savvy friend or practically any teenager to help you with phrasing and exploring the results. (Give yourself a time limit with this research step, so you don't allow this stage to linger for a year or something. Anywhere from a few days to a couple weeks is probably reasonable.) Here are some questions to get you started on your research:

Who is my market? (Who will really love this and buy it? Better yet, who would I *love* to have buying it and talking about it?)

What similar items are out there already, and how is mine unique? (If I imagine people gushing to their friends about my pieces, what are they saying?)

What is a price point that will feel like a good value to buyers but still allow me to maintain a profitable business? (What price feels good to me? At what price do I feel both valued and guilt free?)

How are other people selling stuff like this? Art fairs? Websites? Parties? From the back of their cars? Local stores or boutiques? (Do I like the way they're doing it? How would I do it better? What do I want right now—*a higher* *yield per piece*, doing more myself, or a *higher volume of sales,* requiring more outside involvement and support? Which will get me closer to what I really want from the experience?)

How involved do I want to be with the day-to-day stuff—the manufacture, packaging, mailing, client communication? (What are the skills I'd like to apply? What's the stuff I can't stand doing? Where am I intimidated? Confident?)

Where are my resources richest? Where are they most limited? (Do I have plenty of pieces ready but little money for promotion? Can I barter goods or services? Do I have plenty of money but no time to assemble things? Can I hire help?)

Once you've established your desires around your art pieces, find some context on your industry or field. You might start by going to a Web search engine (like Google) and simply type "sell my crafts," "self-publish my book," "sell my paintings online," or whatever it is you'd like to accomplish. Sift through results carefully before getting out the credit card. There will be sites pressuring you to buy a very expensive, hyped-up "secret" system for successfully getting your work out to market. Skip these. Established, reputable companies will happily provide clearly outlined services (along with tons of support) for typically modest fees. There are many established sites set up for the express purpose of helping independent creators develop and sell their wares. They'll be invested in your success and will usually offer many free resources for maximizing your sales. Here's a sampling of reputable sites for different genres.

Etsy.com (art pieces, clothing, crafts, and much more)

Amazon.com (publish and sell through the CreateSpace and Advantage programs)

Lulu.com (self-published books, photography books or portfolios)

ArtistRising.com (print-on-demand artprints of photos or paintings)

CafePress.com (merchandise with your artwork or text on it)

Taxi.com (song placements and opportunities for songwriters/musicians—an excellent resource)

CDBaby.com (sales of independent music or spoken word CDs—another excellent resource for independent musicians)

Alamy.com (licensing images, stock photography)

Photoshelter.com (commercial photo licensing, print-on-demand prints)

Lastly, rack your brain and come up with anyone you know—and I do mean *anyone*—involved with the field you're entering. Contact them and ask if you might ask them a few questions. Tell them you're just getting started and you'd really appreciate their advice. Everyone likes feeling like an expert, so if you frame it well, you'll probably get a positive response. So when they agree to talk with you or meet for a coffee or lunch, jump through all the appropriate hoops. Be prompt, upbeat, conscious of their valuable time, gracious and nice, and resist the nervous tendency to act as if you already know everything (or to waste time talking about yourself). Keep financial questions—if you must ask them—as general as possible. If your contact offers to help you connect with other people who might be helpful or have ideas for you, follow up on the opportunity while the offer is fresh—say, within a week or two at most. After your meeting, send a thank-you note (email is also okay, but not as special).

Keep your desired end result in mind throughout the journey. Be bold enough to have an intention for each step of the way. Don't freak out if you feel a little nervous as you reach out to people or organizations that intimidate you. Nervousness is as rich a source of energy as there is. Put it to good use; redirect it into the feeling you'd like to experience after the interaction.

Q: "People tell me that I have a good voice, and I love singing. Other than karaoke—or a community choir, which isn't really my bag—how can I find a way to get out and sing more?"

A: The good news is that you've got a clear idea of what you want (music in your life) and what you don't (karaoke or a local choir). Go a step further: what else would you like to get out of a regular singing experience (or other art experience, if you're reading this from a nonmusical perspective)?

Nervousness is as rich a source of energy as there is. Put it to good use; redirect it into the feeling you'd like to experience.

First, decide how you'd like to feel. Maybe you'd like the kick of singing in front of a lively crowd, the fun of being the center of attention, the opportunity to explore a different part of yourself.

Ask what your strengths are, both musical and otherwise. Do you have an angelic soprano? Are you naturally well organized? Can you read music? Can you commit to a rehearsal schedule? Do you have some original songs you might like to develop? Are you interested more in the experience than the money?

Now write up a "universal want ad" in your journal, listing your strengths and exactly what your ideal situation would be. Here's an example: "Easy-going thirtyish female lead singer with a velvety alto seeking bluesy group to play with for fun, mellow gigs a few times a month." (Be as detailed as possible!)

Trust that your clear desire will set things in motion. Start watching for opportunities. *Someone* is looking for somebody exactly like you! Check listings in the free weekly papers (every large city has them) and online classifieds, too. (Sites like *craigslist.org,* or *kijiji.com* have tons.) If you don't see the perfect situation, go ahead and actually place your ad in the "musicians and bands wanted" section, and let them come to you.

Get out in your local community. You might be able to belt out a song like Celine Dion, but no one's going to find you in your shower stall. Get thee to an open mic and get thy ass up there (if

you can sing a cappella or accompany yourself). Get out and meet people.

If you're a writer, look for a local writing group or attend readings of authors you like. Other artists might discover a local photography club, cooking school, art association, local TV station, or community dance center to join, attend, or support.

Let people know what kind of opportunity you're looking for. (And, again, for goodness sakes, if someone suggests a contact for you to call, do it! I can't believe how often people sit on the exact information they need because they're a little intimidated.)

Now go kick some ass.

Q: "Sometimes I get confused by my own *wants!* I think I want one thing, then I'm not sure, then I think I want a different thing. I'm not sure what's draining and what's amping me up; I just know I'm feeling uneasy. I know that having my attention bounce from thing to thing isn't helpful. Any suggestions?"

A: Have you heard of *muscle testing?* One way to check your desire level or energy is to note a sense of expansion/contraction in your body and vibe through a form of muscle testing or energy-field awareness. Give it a try. Stand up, close your eyes, and think of the project at hand. Think of each option you're considering, one at a time, and check each choice against your physical and subtle energetic response.

Notice what your body does. Do you feel a subtle clenching or tightness in your gut, jaw, neck? Does your posture change to a less stable, less powerful position? Do you feel like you're tipping backwards? Do you feel any physical discomfort or stress, such as an elevated heart rate or breathing pattern, increased sweating, or an urge to move or get away from this thought or location? Do you experience a sense of being mentally scattered? These are all signs that you're rejecting this choice.

Do you feel relaxed and focused, with a warmth in your hands or feet? Are you holding a comfortable, powerful posture or stance, or feeling as if your weight is pitching you forward? Do you feel more at ease? If you close your eyes and smile as you think about the possible project, does this feel natural and unforced? In this case, your energetic feedback is giving you the go-ahead.

Another way to sense an energetic response is to imagine that you've placed dots or beads on the edge of your personal energy field, and you can see it or feel it moving. As you consider your options one at a time, do you have a sense of this field collapsing toward you, caving in on itself? Or is it growing more open, wider, expansive? As you may have guessed, contraction means no and expansion means yes.

There are also quick, subtle ways to muscle test using finger holds or resistance against a raised arm. Find much more information by doing an Internet search for "muscle testing" or asking for guidance from a chiropractor, massage therapist, or energy worker who uses the technique in his or her practice.

Q: **"I've tried so hard to get my book published, and all I've gotten is rejection after rejection (and a tiny bit of constructive criticism). How do I know when to keep the faith or move on?"**

A: Energetically, let's open you up a little. There's always a core desire at the heart of our efforts. What do you *really want* to get out of having your book published? What do you hope to *feel* then? Valued? Insightful? Talented? See if you can narrow your hopes down to the essence of what you really want.

Is your core desire about external validation (you want an industry professional to tell you you're talented)? Is it about completion (it just won't feel done unless it's out there and available to readers) or money (you want to bring in income with your art form)? Do you want the guidance or resources (you have no idea how to market or distribute a book and would like experienced help)? There are dozens of possibilities, so take some time to identify what you, deep down, expect to gain from having your book published.

Are there other places in your life where you recognize this core desire as an issue? (Here's a hint: yes.) Can you expand upon the areas where it's working well and allow that vibe to spill over into your publishing quest? Figuring out what you want from the publishing process (and which parts of the process you're willing and excited to do yourself) will help you sort out your choices.

In practical terms, you do have options other than (1) continuing to bang your head against a wall and (2) giving up. If you believe your book is ready and that there are people who will want to read it, there are ways to effectively get your book into readers' hands. You could choose to self-publish, publish digitally, or establish a print-on-demand arrangement. You might also consider working under the model of "partner publishing," where you participate in the efforts (and cost) of getting your book designed, printed, distributed, and promoted. (Sometimes this is called "vanity publishing," but don't let that term deter you. This option can work quite well and offer quite attractive per-book returns compared to other publishing models.)

You have options other than (1) continuing to bang your head against a wall and (2) giving up.

You can attend writers' conferences where you might find more plentiful feedback on what's effective (or not) in your book. You also may meet potential agents or publishers who will help you move forward with the publishing process of your choice, or find peers with whom you could start a writing group.

I'll hope to be reading your book soon, one way or another!

Q: "I think it would help if I had someone to represent my work. When is it time to get an agent? How do I get a good one?"

A: Well, the big joke is that you can get an agent the moment you don't need one anymore. Consider the basic economics: most agents make only 10 to 20 percent of what you make. If you're not yet making a good living from your art, 10 to 20 percent of that amount isn't much. Additionally, it's often the least-established artists who require the most work and guidance (for the least amount of financial return).

The big joke is that you can get an agent the moment you don't need one anymore.

However, you've got options. It always comes back to desire. "What do you want?" and "Why do you want it?"—these are the questions that help us distill external desires down to the feelings we want. So ask yourself *why* you really want an agent. Do you want someone speaking for you? Do you feel you can't keep up with all the work? Do you hope they'll drum up more work for you? Do you need better contacts?

If you're just getting started, your best bet might be to enlist the skills of an enthusiastic friend who wants to help. Many professional agents actually got started this way. Enthusiasm and devotion go a long way toward learning the business and promoting a client.

You may also choose to do agent tasks yourself. There are rich resources available now that were not accessible even a few years ago. A brief exploration online can yield submission guidelines, contact information, public-relations expectations, and other requirements related to pitching yourself for a specific gig. If you've got a good business sense and can speak or write well, it might be quite straightforward to handle things on your own for a while.

Lastly, you could read trade journals or buy books of industry addresses, and get in contact with established agents until your persistence, talent, or growing resumé elicits a call back. Figure out which agencies do what you're seeking and which ones might be most likely to work with you at your present level. Take note of any "dream agencies" you discover, too—just in case.

A good way to target appropriate agents is to find out who represents artists similar to, but not exactly like, you—at a level *at, or just above,* where you are. Think like the agency: if they already have someone like you, they don't need another one. But they might need a complement to one of the artists on their roster, however. Would you be a perfect opening act for someone they represent?

A note on targeting: please, *I beg you,* be selective. Contact only a few agents at a time. Do *not* waste trees or clog up Internet bandwidth by sending packets, emails, or electronic press kits to everyone in a professional listings book! By targeting and being selective, you'll get better response (and you'll know who the hell someone is if you do get a call back). Additionally, since you'll have prescreened the people you contact, you can be confident that if you *do* hear from someone on your list, it's an agent who's likely to be a good fit.

Last word: if you have something major happen (like, "Hey! I'm going to be on *The Oprah Winfrey Show* tomorrow! Yay!"), there is a great, mystical, brief window that opens, and you'll find that almost any agent will consider taking you on. If you've become familiar with your dream agency in advance, it'll be easier to take advantage of these kind of wonderful opportunities in a way that provides long-term value for both parties. (Remember how we explored getting ready for your Big Gig, back in Chapter Twelve? This is exactly the kind of breakthrough moment that benefits from your visualizing and advance preparation!)

Q: There seems to be a lot of conflicting advice about energy, focus, and intention. Here are some of the things I've heard and find confusing:

1. **"Be specific"/"don't designate your source."**
2. **"Set a time frame on your goal"/"let the universe work on its own timeline."**
3. **"Think about it several times a day, focus on it regularly"/ "just send it out there and forget it" (continuing to think about it shows a lack of faith that your desire is coming).**
4. **"Resist the urge to water down your intention by talking about it"/"declare your intention often and publicly."**

A: With each of these options, choose the one that *feels good for you*. When you're at a crossroads with an approach, choose the option that makes you feel *great*—full of excitement, expectation, anticipation, delight, or even a calm certainty. For each of us, there is one of the above choices in each conflict that feels better and makes more sense to us than the other. This is the way to go.

Remember when we discussed vision boards and affirmations, and how they work sometimes, but not as well as many of us might like? It's the same thing here. If your approach stokes the furnace of great feelings, you're on the right track. Go for it, no matter what any rules might say. Conversely, if you *don't* find yourself with enhanced, elevated feeling states taking place, you won't see the results you want, no matter what method you're using.

Creative Soul Search

The first thing I'm inspired to do next for my work is ______________________________
____
____

When I will start: ______________________________ (date).
I'm daunted by the research question about ______________________________
____
____

I might be able to find some answers by ______________________________
____
____

I'm excited to check out ______________________________ (website or organization). I bet they might be able to help me ______________
____
____

If I absolutely *had* to, I could probably contact ______________________ ______________________ and ask for some advice and guidance.

Or at very least, ______________________ might know someone I could ask.

I could probably take the big step of ______________________________
____
____

if I tried ______________________________
or asked ______________________________
or stopped ______________________________
or believed ______________________________

My universal want ad would have to include the following five things about my ideal situation: ______

A conflict I was caught up on about energy is ______

The feel-good option or resolution for it is ______

I thought my desire to ______ was so I could ______

But I think it might actually be more about ______

I'm thankful for ______

CHAPTER FIFTEEN

Kick-Ass Creative for Life

How can you hold onto the sparks of positive energy and great ideas you've discovered in yourself? How can we implement focus as a daily part of life, as a wonderful lifelong practice?

Get out your calendar, planner, phone, or event-management program on the computer. We've got some planning to do for the next couple months. It's time to implement, baby! We'll add levels, week by week, continually layering new elements to the practices from the week(s) before. In no time, you'll find you're happier, luckier, making more money, finding better parking places, getting better jobs, and attracting whatever else you desire.

Start right now. This moment. *Decide that conscious, creative focus is going to be habit.* Intend and expect that you'll feel better and see better results by applying your focus to only that which you want, enjoy, or wish to expand. Decide that you will look for and find evidence that your conscious focus is working effectively in your life.

Week One: Become hypervigilant about positive focus. Avoid getting sucked into your negative thoughts and feelings. The moment you feel one comin' on, high tail it *out* of there and shift toward something that sounds more inviting. Refuse to engage with automatic negative thoughts, and release any so-called practical attachment to old (negative) assumptions and filters. You do not need negativity in order to analyze your life or see things "realistically." You need only your connection to Source, a beautifully protective, positive vibe, and your clear, unfettered intention toward the results you want. Jot down something like "Fiercely positive!" on your calendar for these days.

Week Two: Give yourself ten minutes of sitting in silence each day. Meditate, ground yourself, pray, open up to contact from your creative team, or just sit. Make room in your busy, chaotic day for ten minutes of easy access to your creative spiritual energy. Big Creative just might have a big present for you. Keep a notebook handy in case you feel the cheery knock of inspiration. Notate calendars with something like "Shh."

Week Three: Energize your day with a morning intention ritual. As you become conscious while lying in bed in the morning, decide what you'd like to attract or accomplish for the day. If you don't have a clear idea of something to attract, ask the universe to indicate how you might serve your greatest purpose today. Do a mini grounding exercise to balance and enhance your energy before getting up, and finish with bright white sparkling light filling your body and expanding all around you. Your calendar code might be "Know and glow."

Week Four: Nurture your gratitude. Choose at least one of the following practices to adopt every day. Before you drift off to sleep, think of five things for which you're thankful. If you can write them down in a gratitude journal, even better. If you use a social-messaging network, use it; become the Facebooking fairy of gratitude, the Tweet-queen of thankfulness. If you write a blog, conclude it with five things for which you're most thankful today. Give thanks before your meals if you've gotten out of the habit or like the idea. Write an actual thank-you note and mail it to someone. Jot down "Thx!" on your calendar days.

Week Five: Devote fifteen minutes of your day to new or neglected projects. Decide which projects sound most exciting and interesting to you right now, and start there. You might choose to be *practical* (clearing off your beloved old writing desk), *research oriented* (using the time for Web searches or reading up on a topic), *engaged in your form* (writing, dancing, painting, reciting monologues), *interchange oriented* (writing thank-you notes or contacting possible mentors, entering competitions), or *personal and thoughtful* (journaling or scripting). Anything that feels good, and feels like progress, is perfectly acceptable. Calendar code: "Power 15."

Week Six: Eliminate drains and tolerations. On the first day of the week, keep a notebook with you and jot down any tolerations you notice. Anywhere you experience your energy or mood taking a dip, note what you feel is causing the reaction. (Don't freak out if your list is quite long. The first time I did this, mine was six pages.) We've waited this long to get to tolerations because by now you should have a solid foundation in positive focus; you won't get all bogged down by a few things you'd like to adjust and improve. Over the week ahead and following weeks, address a couple tolerations each day. Choose tolerations that dovetail with your energy level and enthusiasm for the particular day. Tuckered out? Try some little baby tolerations. Big wave of get it the hell done? Approach some whopping big tolerations! *Obliterate* those suckers! On the calendar: "Banish drains."

Week Seven: Do an *energy inventory* on day one. How are you feeling? What's working and helping? What feels better than it has in ages? What isn't contributing to a better state for you? Which habits and energy work do you wish to let go of, and which can you embrace more excitedly? What's happening with your creative work? Are you receiving any feedback from people in your life about your apparent vibe or mood? Throughout the rest of the week, apply the changes based on what's feeling good and what's not. If you've put off doing some of the exercises, questions, or

project recs, use this week to journal and work on them to help fine-tune areas needing special attention.

Week Eight: Gather up any notes with inspired ideas and potential actions, and start planting some seeds and watering any happy little seedlings that have begun to grow. Nurture your expectation by writing notes, entering competitions, showcasing your work in new places. Create a constant, loose state of possibility and fun. Then, start scripting. Choose two—just two—areas of your work and life upon which to shower your attention for the next month. Use all your tools—everything you've got. Write in your journal, make a vision board, meditate, talk about it, daydream about it, walk—do whatever it takes to really *feel it.* Get yourself into a vibrant, realistic, sensory feeling place of these two desires. And start watching the changes take place throughout your life. Write on your calendar: "Kick some *ass.*"

And onward. As you grow more empowered and energized, cycle again through the steps (especially in Weeks 5 through 8) at your own pace. Expand your daily creative time commitment. Eliminate more drains and tolerations. Check in with yourself and address personal energy issues as they arise, and revisit exercises and questions that resonate with you. Take on additional focus areas. Keep your momentum!

Or do it *your* way, you creative powerhouse. When you feel like doing *something*, but you're not sure what, open this book to a random page and see what grabs you. Let it speak to you from the shelf some day when you're in a moment of pause. (I'm not proud: keep it with your throne literature if that will get you to pick it up now and again.)

Just *use* the information that has resonated with you. Please, take this opportunity to make the changes you feel inspired to make, to begin implementing the practices that speak to you. Don't fold up your potential and leave it to idle again as you close the book. Your creativity hangs in the balance of your energetic habits. The world *needs* your contribution. You have your unique gifts and ideas for a *reason.*

Your kick-ass creative self is ready to emerge.

Make it so.

STAGING YOUR BIG REVEAL:

Parting Words of Wonder and Hope

Congratulations, artist.

Good job. You made it—you're on your way. (I can feel your spectacular vibe from here!)

It takes courage to step into the bigger shoes of our hopes and dreams. It takes boldness to risk, to explore new ways of approaching something as dear and intimate to us as creating. It takes honesty to look at our long-held habits and patterns with an objective eye, and strength and effort to make the changes that those observations require from us.

And you're doing it! You're leaping!

You've undertaken an energetic makeover that opens the door for higher, clearer creative energy for the rest of your life! Rock *on.*

These techniques take practice, but you'll get them down. Your willingness to press the start button began a journey that will take you exactly where you wish to go. I can't wait to see what you'll do.

See? You *are* a brilliant, kick-ass creator.

(I knew it.)

APPENDIX

Meditations

The following meditations are my interpretations of traditional energy-grounding and chakra exercises. Try making a recording of them,[18] so you fully engage with the process, instead of trying to do it while reading along.

Begin either meditation by settling into a comfortable spot where you won't be disturbed. It's helpful to sit upright with a straight, but relaxed, spine. I find a good time to do either of these is upon waking in the morning. I'll sit right up against the headboard of the bed and use pillows to help me find a supported, comfortable position.

Grounding Circuit Meditation

Close your eyes and begin to breathe deeply. With each breath *out,* allow your energy to effortlessly flow down through the bottom of your spine. Feel it sink down, down, deep

18. Expanded versions of these meditations are available as mp3 downloads at *www.creativelifelabs.com.*

into the center of the earth. Sense your energy wrapping its long, reaching tendrils securely around the earth's core.

Now with each breath *in,* feel your energy flow back up the vinelike path, back to your body, strengthened and enriched by the power of the deep earth—the dense, rich, solid earth. Feel your energy flow back up into your body, filling it until the energy begins to float right up and out the top of your head, floating higher, up toward the sky as you breathe out. With every exhalation, send it even higher, above the clouds and into the open starry universe. Allow your spirit to be energized and refreshed by the open, loose energy of the starry sky, where ideas and inspiration flow easily, happily, lightly across your consciousness.

Now as you breathe in, allow your energy to flow back down into your body via the top of your head. With the next several breaths, create a connected loop as you drop down, down, down with your exhale, and then come back up into your body with the inhale. You are a long, narrow figure eight, breathing in and up, then back in and down, in a continuous loop.

Continue breathing in this circuit until you feel calm sense of being suspended between earth and heaven. You are a spiritual being in a physical body. You are a physical manifestation of spiritual energy. You are connected to both your fully expanded and uniquely individual self. Feel your body fill with expansive, loving knowledge and awareness.

Finish by drawing yourself into your body from both above and below, and taking a long final inhale and exhale to signify your readiness to step back into regular life rhythms.

Chakra Meditation

Start by reminding yourself that you have a direct line to Source and that before you came to this earth, you decided to act as a portal for ideas and inspiration.

First feel the root chakra, a searing ruby red globe of light at the base of your spine, opening and clearing. Feel it opening, expanding, pulsing as it releases any constrictions. Any residual energy that no longer serves you is swirling away, flowing out and away from the base of your spine and dissipating into thin air. Imagine clear, sparkling water flowing over the red light of your root chakra, leaving it sparkling with fresh, clean, beautifully grounded energy. The first chakra grounds us and helps us feel connected with the earth and our physical selves, offering stability and certainty. You are stable, grounded, sure of your place and value in this world. You are enough.

Next feel the second chakra, a brilliant, radiant orange light in the area between your sacrum and navel, opening and clearing. As the second chakra opens and clears, creativity is freed. Magnetism and sensuality increases. Allow the image of clean, shimmering water to rinse away anything that you no longer need or wish to carry, leaving this beautiful, flaming orange blossom to send its radiant energy throughout your body. You supply exciting valuable contributions to the world and to those around you. You are desire in physical form.

Move to the third chakra, a glorious yellow energy center in the middle of your body at the solar plexus. The third chakra offers us access to our full power and strength in this world. Feel it as a yellow, pulsing light as it is cleared of all old and finished energies, all residue of past situations. You can accomplish whatever you desire, whatever you conceive. You are respected. You matter.

Now move up to the fourth chakra, a magnificent, clear green ball of light in the center of your chest, at the level of your heart. Heaviness or cloudiness dissipates as you feel all regret, frustration, or hurt lifting away, leaving your heart chakra in its natural state—bright, bold, open, and the shimmering natural green of forests and grassy meadows. Love physically resides here in the body—love for others, love for self—along with gratitude, shared excitement, compassion, and generosity. By clearing and releasing our heart chakra, we feel a deep acceptance of ourselves and others. You are a special, unique spirit, deeply loving and deeply loved.

Now move to the fifth chakra, a bright blue ball of energy in the area of the throat. Feel as the throat chakra releases all old layers of

communication and information, leaving it clear and sparkling, a vessel for pure truth. When energy flows easily through the throat chakra, we feel relaxed and at ease with speaking and hearing the truth. We float above issues of ego and fear, and become a portal for spirit, a rich channel for wisdom and insight for others, with incredible clarity and certainty for ourselves. You express your ideas and thoughts freely and beautifully. Your voice is heard. You contribute.

Feel your attention lift to the sixth, or "third eye" chakra in the forehead area. A rich, deep, shimmering purple, the third eye chakra houses our wisdom and higher-self insights. Release any heaviness or residue, feeling any uneasiness lift away. When the sixth chakra is clear and bright, we are wide open to direct inspiration, to instantaneous manifestation and synchronicity. You perceive beyond the traditional senses, enhancing your healing, artistic, and observational abilities. You sense a larger picture, absorbing the mosaic of life before you. You see.

Move for a moment to the ear chakras, two disclike energy centers located above your physical ears and a few inches toward the center of your brain. Imagine gently wiping them down with an incredibly soft cloth, leaving them shiny and completely clear and open. With the ear chakras open, you are even more receptive to guidance and clarity from your expanded self and Source. You hear truth, even when it is obscured. You take in and distill information with clarity and ease.

Now move to the eye chakras, located inside your head, behind and slightly above your physical eyes. Similarly wipe these discs down with a beautiful, soft cloth, and ask them to open and release any cloudiness, so the result is two sparkling, gleaming discs. With the eye chakras clear and open, we see layers within the reality around us. The veil becomes more transparent. The path becomes clearer. Visualization skills are greatly enhanced, and your ability to bring desires into a physical reality becomes much stronger. You have vision, and you are unafraid.

Lastly we rest on the seventh, or crown, chakra, which floats just above the top of your head, as if your spine continues straight up into a spectacular orb of white, sparkling light. The crown chakra links us to the divine, as our root chakra connects us to the earth and our physical selves. Allow the crown chakra to release all unnecessary energies and residue, leaving only the highest vibrations. With the crown chakra clear, we are one with all that is; we let go of the ego and join the flow of spirit. We are free from over-identification with material things and open to true, unfettered bliss. We release any need to control. We feel ourselves flowing easily, happily, beautifully downstream toward all we desire. You are complete. You are one with all and everything. You know.

Each of your energy centers has now been cleansed, cleared, and opened. Enjoy the ability of energy to move freely and easily through your physical and ethereal body, balanced and free from all blockages or resistances.

Conclude your chakra session by imagining a sparkling, rose-tinged white light washing over your entire body from head to toe, flowing back up your spine and then over your body again, adjusting the dilation of each chakra to the exact perfect level for you at this moment. Feel the protection of the shielding white light as you intend, as my friend Stephanie does, for "only love and light to come into me, only love and light to come out of me."

FURTHER RESOURCES

DRAWING AND PAINTING

Nicolaides, Kim. *The Natural Way to Draw.* Boston: Houghton Mifflin. 1941.

Schmid, Richard. *Alla Prima: Everything I Know About Painting.* South Burlington, VT: Stove Prairie Press. 1999.

WRITING

Goldberg, Natalie. *Writing Down the Bones: Freeing The Writer Within.* Boston and London: Shambala. 1986.

Lamott, Anne. *Bird by Bird: Some Instructions on Writing and Life.* New York: Anchor, 1995.

See, Carolyn. *Making a Literary Life.* Chicago: Ballantine Books, 2003.

Strunk, William, and E. B. White. *The Elements of Style: 50th Anniversary Edition.* New York: Longman, 2008.

Ueland, Brenda. *If You Want To Write: A Book About Art, Independence and Spirit.* Saint Paul, MN: Graywolf Press, 1987.

Music and Stage Performance

Beeching, Angela Myles. *Beyond Talent: Creating a Successful Career in Music.* New York: Oxford University Press, 2005.

Taylor, Livingston. *Stage Performance.* New York: Pocket, 2000.

Ristad, Eloise. *A Soprano on Her Head: Right-Side-Up Reflections on Life and Other Performances.* Moab, UT: Real People Press, 1981.

General Creativity and Life

Allen, David. *Getting Things Done: The Art of Stress-Free Productivity.* Boston: Penguin (Non-Classics), 2002.

Allen, Pat B. *Art is a Way of Knowing: A Guide to Self-knowledge and Spiritual Fulfillment Through Creativity.* Boston: Shambhala, 1995.

Arrien, Angeles. *The Fourfold Way.* New York: Harper Collins. 1983.

Blake, Amanda. *The Creative Family.* Boston: Trumpeter Books. 2008

Cason, Richard D. *Taming Your Gremlin: A Guide to Enjoying Yourself.* New York: Harper & Row. 1983.

Reynolds, Peter H. *The Dot.* Cambridge, MA: Candlewick. 2003.

———. *Ish.* Cambridge MA: Candlewick. 2004.

Inspiration, Energy, and Following Your Dreams

Breathnach, Sarah Ban. *Simple Abundance: A Daybook of Comfort and Joy.* New York: Grand Central Publishing, 1995.

Cameron, Julia. *The Artist's Way: A Spiritual Path To Higher Creativity.* New York: G. P. Putnam's Sons/Tarcher, 1992.

Carter, Karen Rauch. *Move Your Stuff, Change Your Life: How to Use Feng Shui to Get Love, Money, Respect and Happiness.* New York: Fireside, 2000.

Coelho, Paulo. *The Alchemist (Plus).* San Francisco: HarperSanFrancisco, 2006.

Csikszentmihalyi, Mihaly. *Flow: The Psychology of Optimal Experience.* New York: Harper Perennial Modern Classics, 2007.

Ditzler, Jinny S. *Your Best Year Yet!: Ten Questions for Making the Next Twelve Months Your Most Successful Ever.* New York: Grand Central Publishing, 2000.

Elizabeth, Gilbert. *Eat, Pray, Love. One Woman's Search for Everything Across Italy, India, and Indonesia.* New York: Viking, 2006.

Grabhorn, Lynn. *Excuse Me, Your Life Is Waiting: The Astonishing Power of Feelings.* Charlottesville, VA: Hampton Roads, 2003.

Hicks, Esther, and Jerry Hicks. *Ask & It Is Given.* Carlsbad, CA: Hay House, 2005.

Nemeth, Maria. *The Energy of Money: A Spiritual Guide to Financial and Personal Fulfillment.* New York: Wellspring/Ballantine, 2000.

McTaggart, Lynne. *The Intention Experiment: Use Your Thoughts to Change the World.* New York City: Harper Element, 2008.

SARK. *The Bodacious Book of Succulence: Daring to Live Your Succulent Wild Life.* New York: Fireside, 1998.

Sheldrake, Rupert. *The Sense of Being Stared At: And Other Unexplained Powers of the Human Mind.* New York: Three Rivers Press, 2004.

Sher, Barbara, and Annie Gottlieb. *Wishcraft: How to Get What You Really Want.* Chicago: Ballantine Books, 1996.

Sher, Barbara. *Refuse to Choose!: Use All of Your Interests, Passions, and Hobbies to Create the Life and Career of Your Dreams.* Emmaus, PA: Rodale Books, 2007.

Shinn, Florence Scovel. *The Game of Life and How to Play It.* New York: Cornerstone Library, 1925.

Walsch, Neale Donald. *Conversations With God: An Uncommon Dialogue (Book 3).* Charlottesville, VA: Hampton Roads, 1996.

Coaches/Courses/Adventures

www.goodvibecoach.com

Jeannette Maw, Attraction coach/Law of Attraction, author of *The Magic of Pray Rain Journaling.*

www.intuitiondecks.com

Digital widgets, apps, and physical card decks providing action-based suggestions for opening your flow and following your muse!

www.TheArtStudioNY.com

A great school and resource for getaways, art classes, and creative development.

www.creativeweekends.com

Retreats for artists, creatives, and those who want to be.

www.creativelifelabs.com

Creativity-driven downloadable audio scripts/meditations available by topic and genre.

www.corporateshamaninc.com

Consulting and energy-rich programming and retreats for corporations and individuals.

www.wordle.com

Fun with graphic renderings of words.

Give Back, Take Part

www.moreperfectworldfoundation.org

Supporting artistic expression programs as an instrument of renewal and positive social impact.

www.parkcityinstitute.org

Dedicated to fostering creative entrepreneurship.

ACKNOWLEDGMENTS

Thank you to all who made this book possible. I'm thankful for all the good people of Hampton Roads, especially Jack Jennings and Greg Brandenburgh, for your faith and vision. Big thanks to my agent, Teresa Hartnett, for her gracious guidance and help, and to Lynn Grabhorn for writing a book that changed my life in so many positive ways (and helped me find my way to this project).

Thanks to all my dear friends and fellow artists, especially Felice, Paul, Stephanie, and Susan. Extra love goes to Jill for walking through the creative fire beside me with such unshakable faith and helpful ideas. Thank you Lucy Thomas, Dennis Czerny, Pat Misener, and all the other devoted teachers whose guidance spoke to me so often while writing. Thanks, too, to the warm, nurturing coffeehouses where I frequently work; I have taken up many hours at your tables and am so grateful for your hospitality.

My deepest thanks to my wonderful parents, siblings, and in-laws—the whole Gelbuda and Maziarz clans—for supporting my creative pursuits with such trust and enthusiasm, and for taking care of Daisy so lovingly when I needed time to write. (And thanks for taking care of me too!) I truly cannot thank you enough.

Lastly, I thank my little pumpkin, Daisy, for tolerating more hours away from her mom than a toddler would prefer, and my amazing husband, Mark, for the love, support, and creative partnership that keeps our life brimming with excitement, fun, and endless possibility.

About the Author

Mary Beth Maziarz is a professional songwriter and performer whose songs have appeared in over 50 films and television shows. Along with her music work, Mary Beth frequently presents and leads creativity workshops, where she helps both established and emerging creative individuals reach new heights by tapping into unique forms of focus and inspiration. She lives in Park City, Utah, with her husband, photographer Mark Maziarz, and daughter Daisy. This is her first book.

Mary Beth would love to hear about your Kick-Ass Creative adventures.
Visit *www.kickasscreativity*, or write to:

Mary Beth Maziarz
P. O. Box 4093
Park City, UT 84060-4093